500 FACTS

Dinosaurs

www.pegasusforkids.com

© **B. Jain Publishers (P) Ltd.** All rights reserved. No part of this book may be reproduced, stored in a retrieval system or transmitted, in any form or by any means, mechanical, photocopying, recording or otherwise, without any prior written permission of the publisher.

Published by Kuldeep Jain for B. Jain Publishers (P) Ltd., D-157, Sector 63, Noida - 201307, U.P. Registered office: 1921/10, Chuna Mandi, Paharganj, New Delhi-110055

Printed in India

CONTENTS

Preface 5

INTRODUCTION

The Beginning of Life 6

What Is a Dinosaur? 9

Classification 16

Nesting Habits 18

Feeding Habits 19

ORNITHISCHIAN (BIRD-HIPPED) DINOSAURS

Cerapoda and Thyreophora 20

SAURISCHIAN (LIZARD-HIPPED) DINOSAURS

Sauropoda 82

Theropoda 106

AVIAN DINOSAURS

Primitive Feather Dinosaur 133

Non Avian Dinosaur with Feathers 135

Present Day Relatives 144

DINOSAUR EXTINCTION

Causes 150

Early and Late Birds 157

Fossil Records 163

Important Personalities 170

Media on Dinosaurs 181

PREFACE

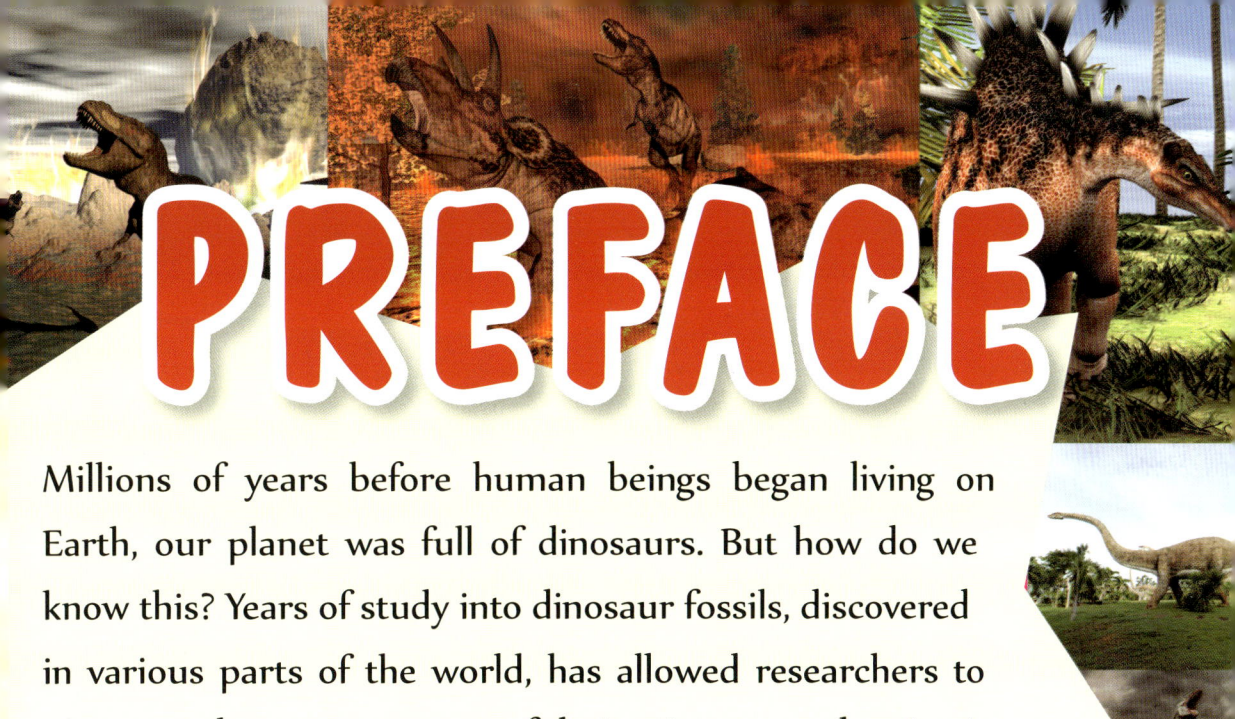

Millions of years before human beings began living on Earth, our planet was full of dinosaurs. But how do we know this? Years of study into dinosaur fossils, discovered in various parts of the world, has allowed researchers to piece together many aspects of their existence and extinction. However, several things about their days on Earth remain unexplained.

It is this mysterious facet of the dinosaurs—their survival, evolution and eventual disappearance—that has fascinated scientists and popular imagination for decades.

500 Facts Dinosaur attempts to bring to the reader whatever is known about the various dinosaurs that once lived on Earth in a fast-facts format. The book aims to enhance your understanding of dinosaurs, and add value to your knowledge.

Happy Reading!

INTRODUCTION

The Beginning of Life

1 You will be amazed to know that the planet Earth was formed by the same process and the same matter and at the same time as other planets of our Solar System. The Sun is the only source that provides energy to these planets, but Earth is the only planet which supports life.

2 Scientists believe that the Earth was formed around 4.6 billion years ago and in the very beginning, there was no life on it. The ground was blistering hot and there was no water, so survival was impossible. A sea of molten rock covered the newly formed Earth.

THE BEGINNING OF LIFE

3 **Do you know how oceans were formed?** As the young Earth cooled down slowly, the scorching steam released by volcanoes condensed to form liquid water that fell as rain. This produced a downpour that lasted for millions of years. More water was brought by comets and asteroids which then pooled on the surface to form oceans.

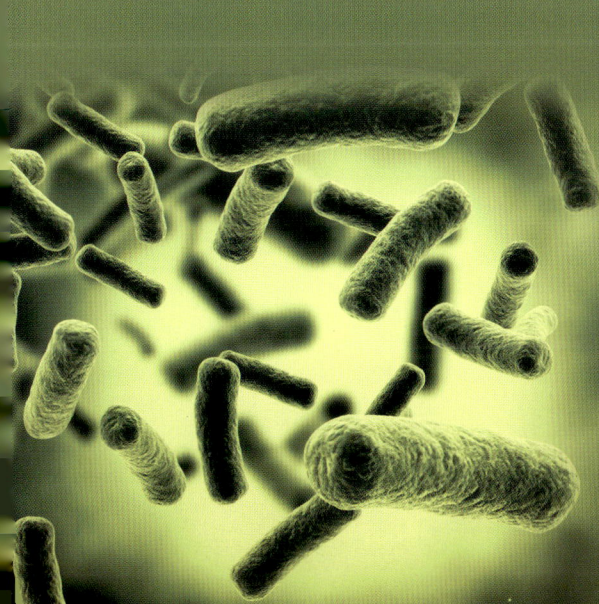

4 **Scientists believe that life in the deep sea began around 3.8 billion years ago.** The Earth's deadly surface was not safe for life, so it is believed that the first life forms might have first emerged around hot volcanic vents. These early microscopic creatures would have fed on energy-rich chemicals dissolved in the boiling water.

INTRODUCTION

5 **Stromatolites are rock-like mounds formed by colonies of bacteria and are the oldest evidence of life on Earth.** Scientists have found fossils of stromatolites dated to around 3.5 billion years old. Did you know that you can still find living stromatolites in the Shark Bay region of Western Australia? Bacteria were the only form of life on earth for around three billion years.

6 **You may know that new species develop from old ones over a period of time.** These new species appear by a process of gradual change called evolution. Evolution takes place through a method called natural selection. Plants and animals produce many offspring from which nature selects the ones that have the best characteristics and passes them on to later generations.

7 **Have you ever wondered from where Earth first got oxygen to support life?** The bacteria in stromatolites live like plants; they use the Sun's energy to make their food and release oxygen during this process. This process produced enough oxygen over a long period of time to increase the amount of oxygen in the atmosphere, paving the way for oxygen-breathing animals to evolve.

What Is a Dinosaur?

8 **Sir Richard Owen in 1842 gave the term 'Dinosauria' to describe fearfully great reptiles.** Till the time only three dinosaurs, specifically Megalosaurus, Iguanodon and Hylaeosaurus were known. Even though dinosaurs are no longer alive, they are considered to be one of the most long-lived groups of animals that have ever survived.

9 **Scientists believe that the origin of dinosaurs occurred between 231-234 million years ago.** For about 135 million years, they roamed the Earth. Dinosaurs were the largest land animals of all time, but not all dinosaurs were so huge. In fact, they ranged in size from animals no bigger than pigeons to lumbering giants the size of trucks.

INTRODUCTION

10 **Dinosaurs differed from today's reptiles and lizards in many ways.** For one, they stood on their legs straight, in the same way as mammals do now. Today's reptiles and lizards cannot stand up straight on their legs whereas some dinosaurs walked on two legs, some on four and some may have done both.

11 **The Mesozoic era lasted for around 180 million years.** In this era, for close to 164 million years, dinosaurs were present on the Earth. At that time, the climate of the Earth was warmer by about 100 degrees Fahrenheit and the continents were shaped differently. During this period, the land masses changed dramatically.

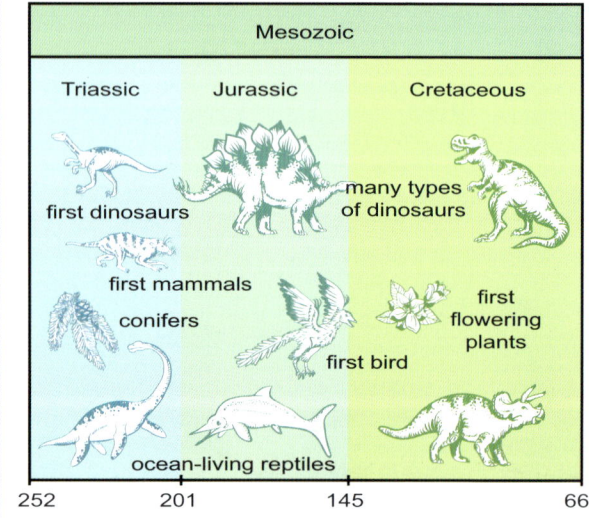

WHAT IS A DINOSAUR?

12 **The Triassic period began about 251 million years ago and lasted for around 50 million years.** During this period, a north-south land mass formed, when all the Earth's continents were joined together. This has been given the name of Pangaea. During this time, the coastal areas and river valleys were green, but much of the interior were made up of deserts.

13 **By the middle of the Triassic era, the Eoraptor and Herrerasaurus evolved as the first true dinosaurs.** The dinosaurs of this era were fairly small in size and they lived in a hot and largely barren world. Some other early dinosaurs were the Plateosaurus, Chindesaurus and Coelophysis.

14 **A tragic event occurred at the end of the Triassic period known as the end-Triassic extinction or Triassic-Jurassic extinction.** This resulted in the demise of around 76 per cent of marine species and around 20 per cent of all taxonomic families. This helped dinosaurs to become the dominant land animals.

INTRODUCTION

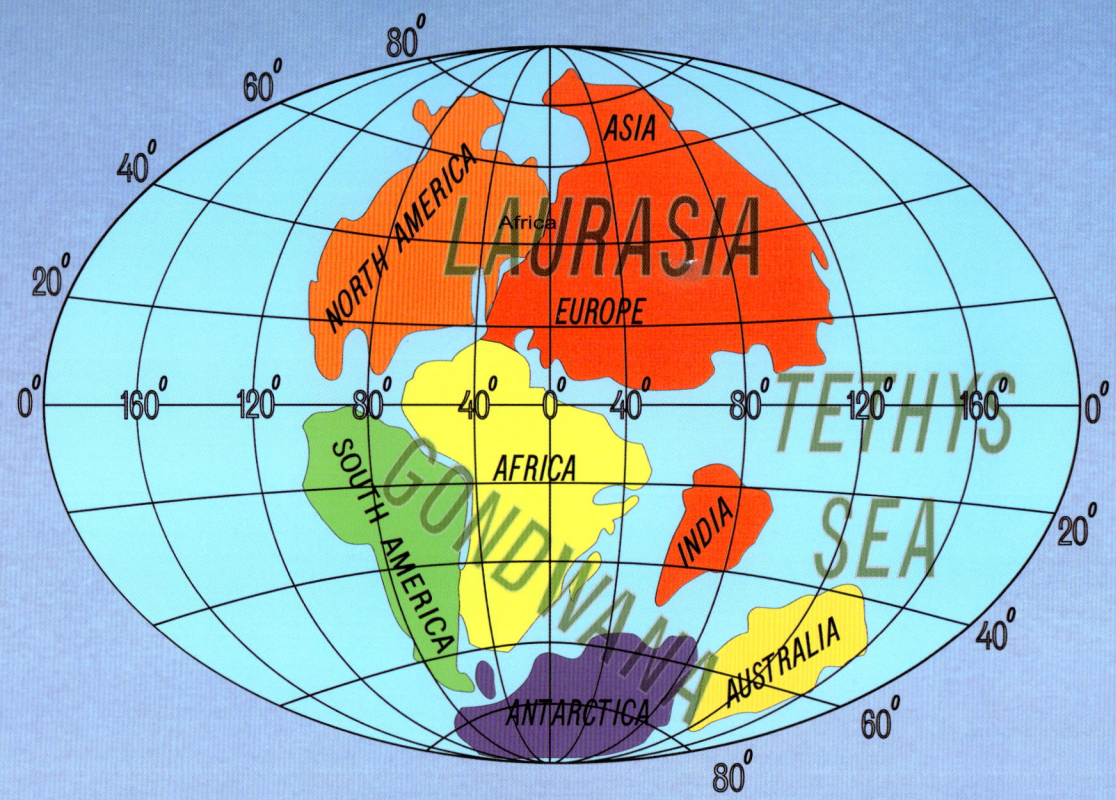

JURASSIC PERIOD

145 MILLION YEARS AGO

15 **The Jurassic period lasted for about 65 million years (200–145 million years ago).** The second segment of the Mesozoic Era, 'The Age of Reptiles', is known as the Jurassic period. During this period, Pangaea (the single landmass) started splitting into two bodies which created Laurasia in the north and Gondwana in the south.

16 **You will be amazed to know that during the beginning of the Jurassic period, there lived small and lightly boned bipedal and carnivorous dinosaurs that depended upon insects and other small dinosaurs for food.** It was during the Jurassic period that there was a dramatic increase in the numbers and variety of dinosaurs.

WHAT IS A DINOSAUR?

17 **Massive dinosaurs, such as the Allosaurus and Ceratosaurus, appeared during the end of the Jurassic period.** These heavy-bodied dinosaurs were predators. They were supported by powerful hind legs and front limbs for grasping and holding prey. For spearing and stabbing they had long and sharp teeth.

18 **Sauropods (the largest of all dinosaurs) and plant-eating dinosaurs like Apatosaurus, Brachiosaurus and Brontosaurus, also evolved during the Jurassic period.** They were enormous and very heavy—they could weigh about 20 tonnes or more! They were quadrupeds with pillar-like legs.

INTRODUCTION

19 The last and longest segment of the three periods of the Mesozoic Era was the Cretaceous period. Scientists have estimated that it began 145 million years ago and lasted for 80 million years. During this period, the landmass on the Earth's surface finally took the shape of the continents as we know them today. Thus, Laurasia and Gondwana broke up into several smaller parts.

20 One of the most fascinating dinosaurs, the Pterosaurs (reptiles capable of powerful flight) evolved in the Cretaceous period. Though in general terms, Pterosaurs are considered to be flying dinosaurs, according to some scientists this is incorrect—they are believed to be flying reptiles. It is thought that Pterosaurs were more closely related to birds as compared with any other living reptiles.

WHAT IS A DINOSAUR?

21 Around 65 million years ago, a mass extinction occurred which ended the Cretaceous period and wiped out most dinosaurs (except for the birds). Though the exact reason for this Cretaceous-Tertiary extinction is not known, scientists have offered many theories, such as climate change, asteroid impact and high volcanism.

Classification

22 **Ornithischian (bird-hipped) dinosaurs are so named because their hip bones were superficially arranged like those of birds.** They also had an extra bone called the predentary at the tip of their lower jaw. However, despite what their name suggests, Ornithischians were not related to birds.

23 **The word Saurischia means 'lizard-hipped'.** These dinosaurs are so named because of the similarity of its hip bones and pelvic joint to that of lizards. Saurischians were the oldest known dinosaurs from the middle Triassic of South America. Saurischians are further divided into two categories known as Sauropoda and Theropoda.

CLASSIFICATION

24 It is amazing to know that birds did not evolve from Ornithischian (bird-hipped) dinosaurs but from Saurischians (lizard-hipped) dinosaurs. Later, some groups of Saurischians (Dromaeosaurids and Therizinosauroids) independently evolved a bird-like pubis arrangement.

25 Scientists consider any species of dinosaurs that possess feathers to be feathered dinosaurs. Evidence that connects dinosaurs more closely to birds emerged by the mid-1990s. You will be amazed to know that according to some scientists, birds may have descended directly from Theropod dinosaurs and hence can be classified as dinosaurs.

Nesting Habits

26 **Like reptiles and birds, dinosaurs hatched from round or elongated, hard, brittle-shelled eggs laid by females after sexual reproduction.** Like bird eggs, these eggs contained an embryo in their membrane. Dinosaurs buried their eggs in nests covered with dirt and vegetation. Modern-day crocodiles use the same technique.

27 Researchers believe that the long-necked Sauropods, the plant-eating Ornithischians and the even lesser developed Theropods had high-porosity eggs and they buried their eggs in nests. Dinosaurs like Maniraptorans, which were more developed Theropods, had eggs with low porosity and might have laid their eggs in open nests.

Feeding Habits

28 **It is believed that while most dinosaurs were herbivores, some were carnivores as well.** Herbivore dinosaurs mainly ate plants, whereas carnivore dinosaurs ate lizards, early mammals, turtles or eggs. Some scavenged dead animals and some even hunted other dinosaurs. It is believed that around 65 per cent of dinosaurs were herbivores and the remaining 35 per cent were carnivores or omnivores.

29 **Hesperonychus is the smallest known North American meat-eating dinosaur.** It was only around 19 inches (50 cm) high and about 1 metre long and belonged to the Velociraptor family. The Hesperonychus ate baby dinosaurs, insects and small animals. Although the Albertonykus was smaller than the Hesperonychus, it cannot be considered the smallest carnivore, as it fed exclusively on termites.

30 **Scientists believe that the Spinosaurus lived on land and in water just like crocodiles and ate fish.** The Spinosaurus was the largest among all the carnivorous dinosaurs and can be called the biggest meat eater. It hunted both aquatic and terrestrial prey.

ORNITHISCHIAN (BIRD-HIPPED) DINOSAURS

Cerapoda and Thyreophora

31 It is really amazing to know that Othnielia (an Ornithopod dinosaur) had five-fingered hands and four-toed feet, all of which were clawed. It was a very fast bipedal creature whose thin legs and stiff tail gave it speed and agility. It lived around 156–145 million years ago in the late Jurassic period.

32 For a long time, scientists believed that the Hypsilophodon was an avid tree climber. It had long fingers and toes which might have enabled it to live in trees easily and its foot suggests that it could grasp and perch easily. But recently it has been found that this dinosaur could easily run at high speed on solid ground.

CERAPODA AND THYREOPHORA

33 **You will be amazed to know that the Hypsilophodon had cheek-like structures.** Though most of the dinosaurs did not bother with chewing, the Hypsilophodon sliced up its prey before swallowing, for which it needed space in its mouth which was provided by cheeks. The shape of its skull and jaws show that the creature had structurally evolved space for this purpose.

34 **You will be amazed to know that although the Jeholosaurus was an Ornithiscian dinosaur with distinctively herbivorous teeth in the back of its mouth, its frontal teeth resemble those of a carnivore.** Due to this feature, it is believed that Jeholosaurus dinosaurs were omnivorous, and either hunted smaller animals or ate plants.

35 **In the year 1973, during a construction activity near the Honghe dam in China, the skeleton of a dinosaur was revealed.** The Zigong Salt Industry Museum was notified and their team salvaged some heavily damaged remains. Professor He Xinlu named it 'Yandusaurus'—'yan' means 'salt' and 'du' is 'capital'. The name was apt, as Zigong was historically the centre of Chinese salt mining.

ORNITHISCHIAN (BIRD-HIPPED) DINOSAURS

36 **The Yandusaurus showed a unique pattern in its teeth: there were parallel vertical ridges, which according to Chinese researchers, is comparable to the fingers of the hand of Buddha statues.** In the middle of its jaw, it had fifteen prominent and large maxillary teeth, which overlapped. The eyes of Yandusaurus were very large and they were fast moving bipedal animals.

37 **Can you imagine a dinosaur jumping on mountains? The Orodromeus means 'Mountain Jumper'.** This dinosaur may have spent its life leaping from rock to rock in search of food. It was about three metre (10 feet) long, but was smaller in comparison with other dinosaurs. It had a toothless beak with which it cut and ate vegetation.

38 **The Orodromeus lived in the late cretaceous period. It had a non-fused wrist and dentary teeth with a vertical occlusion.** Within its mouth it had teeth used for crushing and grinding food, before swallowing. It is believed that Orodromeus were similar to another small ornithopod called Oryctodromeus, the burrowing dinosaur.

39 **It is believed that the Zephyrosaurus (also referred to as the 'westward wind lizard') lived in scattered regions of the present-day USA.** It is a genus of the Orodromin ornithopod dinosaur which existed in the late Cretaceous period, over 145 million years ago. Very little is known about these dinosaurs.

CERAPODA AND THYREOPHORA

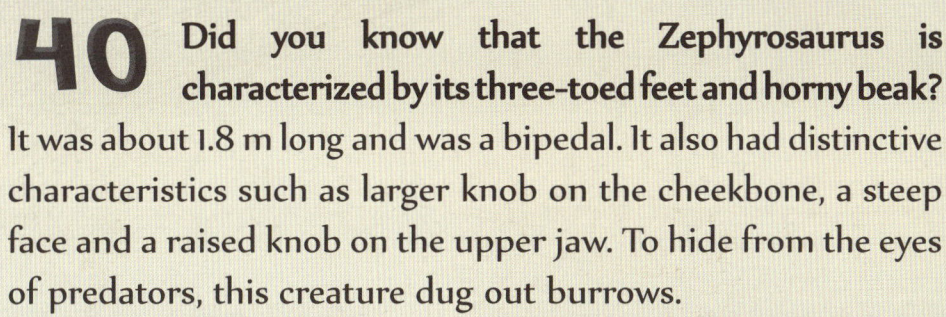

40 Did you know that the Zephyrosaurus is characterized by its three-toed feet and horny beak? It was about 1.8 m long and was a bipedal. It also had distinctive characteristics such as larger knob on the cheekbone, a steep face and a raised knob on the upper jaw. To hide from the eyes of predators, this creature dug out burrows.

ORNITHISCHIAN (BIRD-HIPPED) DINOSAURS

41 Some researchers claim that the Pachycephalosaurs had domed skulls, which in some cases were about eight inches thick and made of brittle bone. Pachycephalosaurs (also known as 'bone heads') were herbivorous and their size varied from small to medium. It is believed that they lived during the mid to late Cretaceous period.

42 Some scientists believe that the round shape of the Pachycephalosaurs' skull helped them during head-butting, as this feature would have lessened the surface area of contact. Another possibility for this round-shaped skull is that it was used as a defence mechanism against predators, as it would have helped in flank-butting. It was also believed that Pachycephalosaurs could make their head, neck and body horizontally straight to transmit stress during ramming.

CERAPODA AND THYREOPHORA

43 **You will be amazed to know that Ceratopsians had huge neck frills and large horns, mainly for display.** They used their hundreds of chisel-edged teeth for slicing through leaves like scissors. They also had hoof-like bones on their fingers and toes. These dinosaurs thrived in the Cretaceous period nearly 80 million years ago.

44 **The Chasmasaurus' neck frills had huge holes that would have been covered by skin.** In order to attract attention or startle enemies, the frill could have been tilted upright and may have been brightly coloured. It is believed that these dinosaurs lived in North America around 74–65 million years ago, in the late Cretaceous period.

45 It is fascinating to learn that the Styracosaurus' magnificent frill sported six spikes, up to 0.6 metres (two feet) long, which may have served as decoration to attract mates. Its sharp teeth could cut through thick vegetation and were constantly being replaced.

ORNITHISCHIAN (BIRD-HIPPED) DINOSAURS

46 **The most remarkable feature of the Pentaceratops was its huge head.** Scientists believe that its skull is the longest of all land animals in history. Pentaceratops means 'five-horned face'—this dinosaur had one horn on the snout, two curved horns on the brow and a small horn on each cheek.

47 **Protoceratops were small Ceratopsians with wide neck frills at the back of their skull that expanded with age.** The frills were larger in males. The Protoceratops had tiny horns between the eyes. They also had broad spade-like claws, which might have been used for digging burrows. It is believed that they mainly lived in Mongolia around 74–65 million years ago.

CERAPODA AND THYREOPHORA

48 The length of the Anabisetia is estimated to have been around two metres and its weight around 20 kilograms. It was a small bipedal herbivore, whose fossilised fragments have been found in South America. In 2010, an American researcher, Gregory S. Paul, studied this unique dinosaur and revealed some strange facts about it. For instance, the connection between the neck and the back of the head of this creature was pointed in a downward direction.

49 One of the species of Anabisetia called 'A. Saldiviai' is named after Roberto Saldivia Blanco, an Argentine farmer who discovered the fossils of the Anabisetia in 1985. It was because of his discovery that scientists came to study this creature in greater detail around 1993. The name 'Anabisetia' was given by Argentine palaeontologist Rodolfo Coria and Jorge Orlando Calvo in 2002.

50 Talenkauen literally means 'small skull'. These dinosaurs seem to have lived primarily in the area of present-day Argentina. An arrangement of oval plates runs alongside the rib cage of the Talenkauen. As these plates seem to be far too few in number to serve a defensive purpose, it is believed they may have aided respiration. To allow the lungs to process a larger volume of air, these plates could have helped in the movement of the rib cage.

ORNITHISCHIAN (BIRD-HIPPED) DINOSAURS

51 An incredible fact about the Triceratops is that scientists have found battle scars in their fossils. Millions of years ago, there seem to have been fierce clashes between Tyrannosaurus and Triceratops, evidenced by bite marks left by the ferocious Tyrannosaurus on some Triceratops' skulls. One Triceratops even seems to have had one of its brow horn snapped off.

52 You will be amazed to know that Triceratops were as heavy as a 10-tonne (9.84207 tonnes) truck. Triceratops got its name because it had a 'three-horned face'—it had a short nose horn and two longer brow horns. Triceratops was built like a huge present-day rhinoceros. This dinosaur used its horns and frills like deer use their antlers, to attract mates.

CERAPODA AND THYREOPHORA

53

The neck of the Triceratops was probably quite flexible which helped them to feed not only on tree leaves but also on low growing plants. They shredded and snipped their food with the help of their scissor-like teeth. They plucked tough forest vegetation with their powerful parrot-like beaks.

54

The Torosaurus were very much like the Triceratops but had larger frills, with openings, or windows. Scientists are unsure whether the two belong to the same species or to different ones. Some even wonder if Torosaurus were mature Triceratops whose shields may have developed the unique windows.

ORNITHISCHIAN (BIRD-HIPPED) DINOSAURS

55 Did you know that there existed dinosaurs whose faces resembled those of horses? Iguanodontians had horse-like faces. They also had huge sails on their backs and beaked mouths for eating plants. They varied from small, nondescript dinosaurs to huge giants. Iguanodontians appeared 156 million years ago in the late Jurassic period.

56 The Iguanodon was the second prehistoric animal to be identified as part of the dinosaur species and was discovered in the 1820s. As the teeth of this dinosaur resembled 'iguana teeth' (though they were around 20 times bigger) it was named Iguanodon. It was as big as an elephant and walked on all four legs; its hind legs were larger and more powerful than its front legs.

CERAPODA AND THYREOPHORA

57 The structure of an Iguanodon dinosaur's hand is really notable. Its three middle fingers joined together to form a hoof. The thumb of an Iguanodon's hand was formed as a vicious spike that might have been for self defence. Also, it could fold its little finger across its palm to grasp objects.

58 The Dryosaurus had a stiff tail to help balance its body while running and may have flicked its tail sideways to make sharp runs to dodge obstacles or outwit pursuers. It had powerful legs that clearly indicate it was a fast runner. It was around three metres (10 foot) long and existed around 155–145 million years ago, in the late Jurassic period.

ORNITHISCHIAN (BIRD-HIPPED) DINOSAURS

59 The Muttaburrasaurus had an arched nose, as the bone forming the top of its snout bulged upward. The size and shape of its snout differed between individuals and probably varied with gender and age. It may have used its large nasal chambers to create honking sounds or to warm the cold air it breathed in.

60 Some dinosaurs are famous for having been 'lunch' for others. The Tenontosaurus was one such unfortunate creatures. Remains of these herbivores are often found within the teeth of smaller, but more ferocious carnivores. They existed in the early Cretaceous period, around 115–108 million years ago.

CERAPODA AND THYREOPHORA

61 A significant trait of the Deinonychus dinosaurs is that they have single, large, curving claws on each of their hind feet. The name Deinonychus is pronounced as 'die-non-ih-kuss'. This dinosaur is considered to be a ferocious carnivore that brought down bigger dinosaurs by hunting in packs; it is also believed that the Deinonychus did not always survive battles with its bigger prey.

62 It is interesting to know that there were dinosaurs whose forelimbs were half as long as their hind limbs and many of them had strangely shaped crests on their heads. The Hadrosaurids, also known as 'duck-billed' dinosaurs, were of this variety. They used their duck-like bills to clip leaves from plants.

ORNITHISCHIAN (BIRD-HIPPED) DINOSAURS

63 **Scientists believe that the Maiasaura dinosaurs looked after their newly hatched offspring rather than leave them immediately upon hatching.** That is why they were named 'Maiasaura' which means 'good-mother'. Bowl-shaped Maiasaura nests have been found close together by scientists in Montana, USA. They think that the site had a nesting colony of Maiasaura, much like the nesting colonies of modern seabirds.

64 **Do you know the Hadrosaurus were the first dinosaurs to be discovered in North America?** Hadrosaurus lived in the late Cretaceous period around 80–74 million years ago. The Hadrosaurus used their toothless beaks to tear twigs and leaves from plants before grinding them to a pulp with the hundreds of tiny teeth located in the back of their mouths.

CERAPODA AND THYREOPHORA

65 **It is hard to believe that the hollow crest of the Lambeosaurus was shaped like a hatchet.** Perhaps this distinctive shape helped this dinosaur to quickly recognise others of its species. The shape of this crest was different in males and females, which suggests that males used their crests to impress female Lambeosaurus.

66 **The Brachylophosaurus had a paddle-shaped crest on its head, a deep snout and a rectangular skull.** Males had wider and heavier crests than females. Brachylophosaurus were about nine metres (30 feet) in length and might have had scaly skin.

ORNITHISCHIAN (BIRD-HIPPED) DINOSAURS

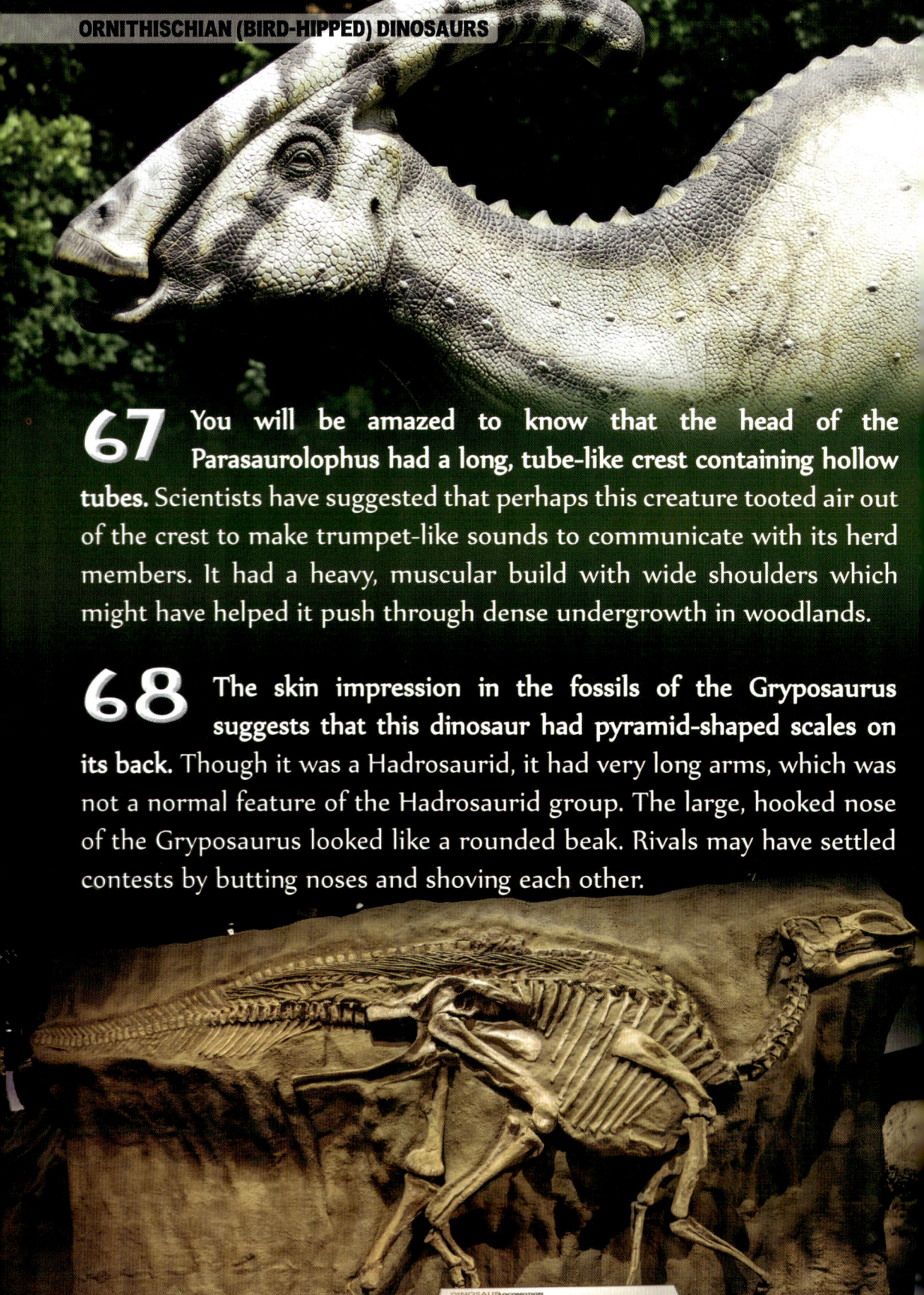

67 You will be amazed to know that the head of the Parasaurolophus had a long, tube-like crest containing hollow tubes. Scientists have suggested that perhaps this creature tooted air out of the crest to make trumpet-like sounds to communicate with its herd members. It had a heavy, muscular build with wide shoulders which might have helped it push through dense undergrowth in woodlands.

68 The skin impression in the fossils of the Gryposaurus suggests that this dinosaur had pyramid-shaped scales on its back. Though it was a Hadrosaurid, it had very long arms, which was not a normal feature of the Hadrosaurid group. The large, hooked nose of the Gryposaurus looked like a rounded beak. Rivals may have settled contests by butting noses and shoving each other.

CERAPODA AND THYREOPHORA

69 **All Hadrosaurids had stiff horizontal tails.** There is an interlocking pattern in their tail bones which prevented their tails from sagging. The shape of the crest of Hadrosaurids would change as they grew into adults. They lived in the Cretaceous period, about 100–65 million years ago.

70 **Several complete skeletons of Corythosaurus have been found in North America.** It is regarded as one of the foremost members of the Hadrosaurid family. The Corythosaurus lived in woodlands covering warm plains near the Rocky Mountains in North America. Its snout was smaller and more delicate than other Hadrosaurids.

ORNITHISCHIAN (BIRD-HIPPED) DINOSAURS

71 The Corythosaurus was one of the larger Hadrosaurids. Tall bony spines on its back were covered with a frill of skin that formed a ridge running along its back. This frill was very prominent at the back of the head, where it was attached. The tubes in the nostrils were connected to its crest.

72 The term Corythosaurus means 'helmet lizard'. Scientists named it so because of the crest on its head which reminded them of helmets worn by the soldiers of ancient Greece. This crested, duck-billed dinosaur is believed to have wandered through woodlands, perhaps in herds, around 75 million years ago. Its crest may have been used as a trumpet to keep in touch with the herd.

CERAPODA AND THYREOPHORA

73 Scientists believe that the crest of Corythosaurus may have worked like a trombone and amplified sounds, helping them to make loud, booming calls that travelled a long way. It is possible that these sounds served as warning signals to alert other herd members about predators lurking nearby.

74 It is really unusual for scientists to find wart-like lumps in a dinosaur's stomach. However, fossils show that the belly of the Corythosaurus had strange, wart-like lumps. Some fossils also had well-preserved impressions of skin on them. The name 'Corythosaurus' was given by Barnum Brown in 1914, based on a fossil found in Alberta, Canada.

ORNITHISCHIAN (BIRD-HIPPED) DINOSAURS

75 Do you know which is the largest duck-billed dinosaur? Edmontosaurus, which was twice the size of a fire engine, was one of the largest duck-billed dinosaurs. It lived alongside other giant dinosaurs, such as Triceratops and Tyrannosaurus, about 66 million years ago. Though it belongs to the Hadrosaurids family, its head had no crest.

76 The Edmontosaurus is named after Edmonton town in Alberta, Canada, where the first fossils of this kind were found in 1917. As one of the largest Hadrosaurids, it weighed up to four tonnes. Hollow areas around its nostrils may have contained inflatable sacs that the Edmontosaurus could expand like balloons and perhaps use to make sounds.

CERAPODA AND THYREOPHORA

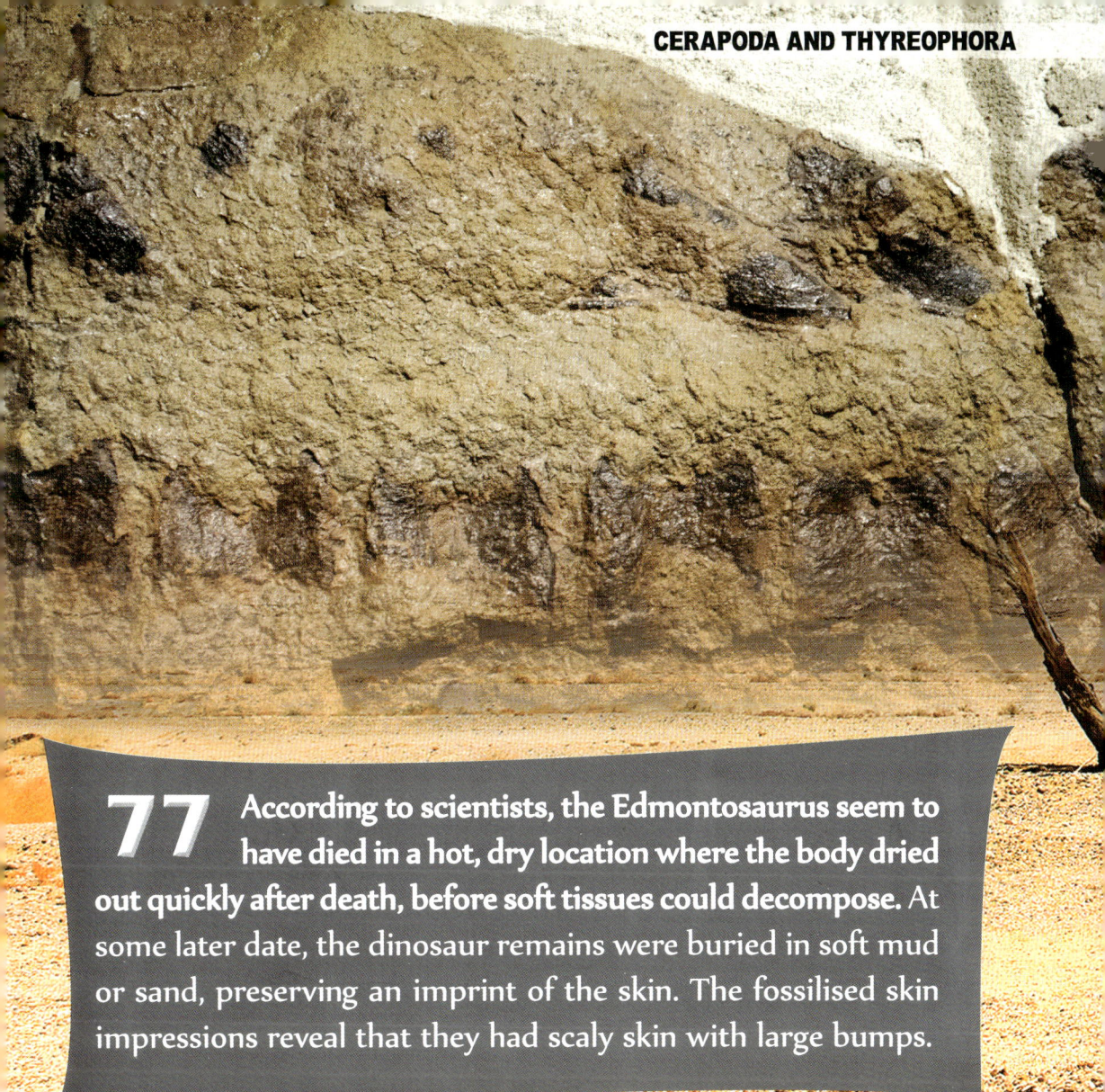

77 According to scientists, the Edmontosaurus seem to have died in a hot, dry location where the body dried out quickly after death, before soft tissues could decompose. At some later date, the dinosaur remains were buried in soft mud or sand, preserving an imprint of the skin. The fossilised skin impressions reveal that they had scaly skin with large bumps.

78 One of the few dinosaurs whose name contains the suffix of the feminine form of lizard—'saura' instead of the masculine form, 'saurus'— is the Gasparinisaura. This name was not given because the type of specimen found was a female, but because the palaeontologist after which this animal is named was a woman—Zulma Brandoni de Gasparini.

ORNITHISCHIAN (BIRD-HIPPED) DINOSAURS

79 **Some animals that lack grinding teeth swallow small stones called gastroliths (stomach stones) to pulverise plant material and aid digestion.** The first, and one of only a handful of non-sauropod herbivorous dinosaurs to be discovered with gastroliths, is the Gasparinisaura. It was first suggested that the dinosaur might have accidentally swallowed these stones, but later discovery of similar clusters in three separate specimens of Gasparinisaura proves this is not accidental.

80 **Researchers believe that the Parksosaurus could hear low-frequency sounds as it had excellent hearing ability.** The Parksosaurus shared the landscape with the Albertosaurus and Pachyrhinosaurus—they all lived in a forested floodplain, dotted with coastal swamps and marshes. It was among the few non-hadrosaurid ornithopods which existed around 70 million years ago, during the end of the Cretaceous period.

Albertosaurus

Pachyrhinosaurus

CERAPODA AND THYREOPHORA

81 **The Parksosaurus had teeth along the sides of its snout, as well as a horny beak at the front of it.** Fossils show that there were bumps known as denticles along the front and back of the teeth of the Parksosaurus, which may have been used to grind plants. In order to extract more nutrients from their food, their lower jaws could move sideways and back and forth while chewing.

82 **The optic nerves in the Hypsilophodontids' brains were very large and that is why it is believed that they had excellent vision combined with large eyes.** There were separate cerebral hemispheres and well-defined optic lobes in the Hypsilophodontid's brain. They had long toes and strong arms for burrowing.

ORNITHISCHIAN (BIRD-HIPPED) DINOSAURS

83 **We know about dinosaurs based on their fossils.** Did you know that there are some dinosaurs that scientists are not sure actually existed? The Kangnasaurus is only known to us on the basis of the remains of one fossil, including a tooth and some leg bones. The lack of more information has made scientists unsure if it should be treated as a separate genus of dinosaur.

84 **The Parksosaurus (which belong to the Hypsilophodont family) are thought to have had hatchlings that weighed between 0.07 and 0.15 kilograms.** Evidence shows that there must have been some level of parental care observed within the nest after birth. It is also believed that like modern-day ground-nesting birds, the Parksosaurus used their nests repeatedly for many years.

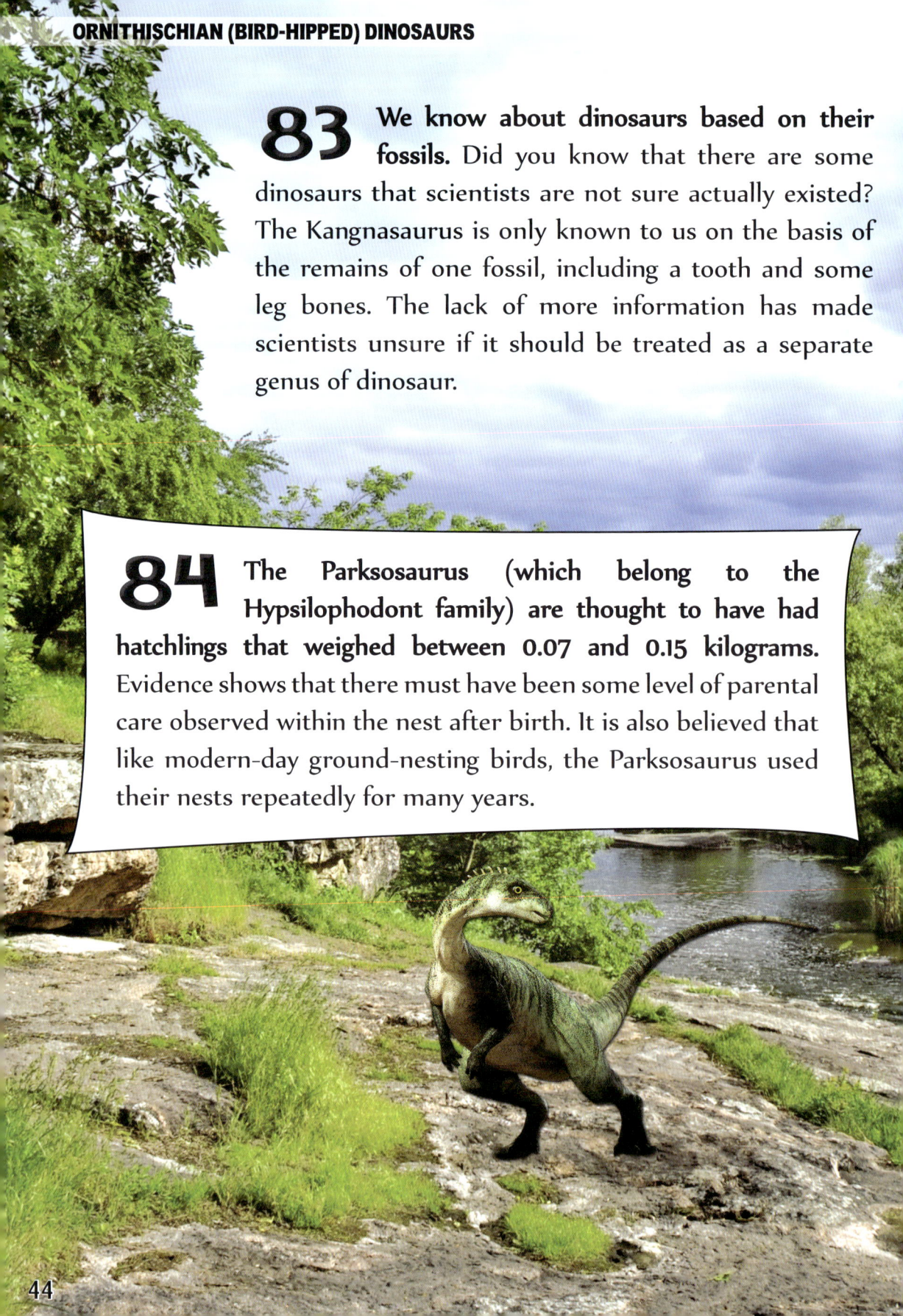

CERAPODA AND THYREOPHORA

85 Even though the Ankylopollexians were herbivorous, they grew to be quite large and are comparable to some carnivorous dinosaurs. Because of their shorter forelimbs, they would stand on all fours while grazing or moving slowly, even though they are considered to be bipedal. It is believed they appeared around 156 million years ago.

86 The name Ankylopollexians is derived from the Greek word 'ankylos' meaning stiff or fused, and the Latin word 'pollex' meaning thumb. The name implies that the creature had a conical thumb spike. The fossils vary greatly in size and the largest known Ankylopollexian is the Shantungosaurus which was about 14.7–16.6 metres in length and weighed almost 16 tonnes.

ORNITHISCHIAN (BIRD-HIPPED) DINOSAURS

87 You will be amazed to learn that the Acrotholus was the oldest confirmed Pachycephalosaur dinosaur from the continent of North America. Like all other known Pachycephalosaurs, the Acrotholus already had a fully developed skull dome. The bone in the dome seems to have been over 0.1 m (10 cm) thick.

88 It is amazing to know that the discovery of Acrotholus is based on two 'skull' caps. One specimen was found by a graduate student of the University of Toronto in the year 2008, while the other was collected by the Royal Ontario Museum over 50 years ago. The Acrotholus audeti was around six feet long and weighed around 40 kilograms.

89 It is interesting to note that the Colepiocephale, though a Pachycephalosaur, had an unusual skull compared with other dinosaurs of its kind—it was not domed or thick, but was flat, sloped and roughly triangular. This was a really tiny dinosaur, around three feet in length and weighed only about 4.5 kilograms.

CERAPODA AND THYREOPHORA

90 Can you believe that the name of a member of the dinosaur family is based on the academy for wizards in the Harry Potter novels? A team of scientists named a dinosaur species 'Dracorex Hogwartsia', which means the 'Dragon king of Hogwarts'. This name celebrates the Hogwarts School of Witchcraft and Wizardry from the Harry Potter series.

91 **Dracorex Hogwartsia closely resembles a dragon: with its bony head covered in spikes and knobs.** Though this dinosaur belongs to the Pachycephalosaur family, it lacks the dome characteristic and is believed to have been herbivorous with a skull sporting spiky horns, bumps and a long muzzle.

ORNITHISCHIAN (BIRD-HIPPED) DINOSAURS

92 The Goyocephale belongs to the Pachycephalosaur family. Its name is derived from the Greek language and means 'adorned head'. The head of the Goyocephale had rudimentary ornamentation and its relatively primitive skull was punctuated by noticeable holes. Though it weighed between 22.5 to 45 kilograms, it had a slim build.

93 Have you heard about the practice of head-butting among dinosaurs? Do you think it was dangerous? The same thought arose in the minds of scientists when they discovered Homalocephale of the Pachycephalosaur family. The broad, flat skull of the Homalocephale was not hard or rigid, instead it was made of prorous bones, interlaced with blood vessels.

94 Scientists came up with two theories regarding the lifestyle of Homalocephale. The first theory is that this dinosaur gave birth to live offspring, as the pelvis of this dinosaur was wide and the extra space between the hips could allow for gestation of foetus. However, there is no proof to back this theory. The second theory is that the wide hips allowed for 'flank-butting' as the internal organs sat further back in the body.

95 It is really ironic that one of the smallest dinosaurs ever discovered has been given the longest name. Micropachycephalosaurus, which means 'small, thick-headed lizard' is believed to have been just one metre long. Before this dinosaur was discovered, Compsognathus was considered the smallest dinosaur.

96 It was only in 2006 that a scientist named Sullivan claimed that the Micropachycephalosaurus does not belong to the Pachycephalosauridae family. The original specimens were examined further by Butler and Zhao in the year 2008. They also found that Micropachycephalosaurus failed to show any characteristics of the Pachycephalosauridae family.

97 According to scientists, the Sphaerotholus may have been the most widespread of all the Pachycephalosauridae family. It is believed that Pachycephalosaurs roamed the woodlands of Asia and America during the late Cretaceous period. The fossils of the Sphaerotholus from the Campanian of New Mexico to the Maastrichtian of Montana confirm its widespread distribution.

ORNITHISCHIAN (BIRD-HIPPED) DINOSAURS

98 Doctoral student Jason Bourke of Ohio University has suggested that according to his research, the Stegoceras would have breathed more like a bird or reptile and taken longer, deeper breaths. According to him, Stegoceras kept their brains from overheating by cooling cranial blood vessels with each breath. In order to avoid inhaling small airborne objects, this dinosaur might have relied heavily on mucus as it lacked nose hair.

99 A palaeontologist called Eric Snively claimed that inside the dome of the skull of a Stegoceras, four distinct 'zones' of bone were present. He pointed out that one could see alternating layers of stiff and compliant bone in the domes. You can visualise this by imagining these dinosaurs wearing double motorcycle helmets.

100 Some scientists assume that male Stegoceras held their heads and necks parallel to the ground. When they had to attack another dinosaur, they would build up a momentum of speed and ram each other as hard as they could. Stegoceras are characterised by their extremely thick skulls, as the noticeable dome on their head was made of almost solid bone.

CERAPODA AND THYREOPHORA

101 Unlike the meaning of its name, the Stygimoloch (the name means 'horned demon from the river of death') was not really very terrifying. It was named because it looked very much like a demon from Christian art. It was a bone-headed Pachycephalosaur; it had bony spikes on its skull, some of which were around four inches long.

102 The Tylocephale, which was only around 1.4 metres in length, had the tallest head dome amongst all of the known Pachycephalosaurs. These were herbivorous dinosaurs, which lived around 75 million years ago, in the late Cretaceous period. It was discovered in Mongolia.

103 You will be amazed to know that the Heterodontosaurus (which means 'different-toothed lizard') had three types of teeth, unlike other dinosaurs who had only one. Its sharp front teeth snipped off tough vegetation. It also had large, fang-like teeth to defend itself from enemies. Its jaws were tipped with a horny beak that was probably used for plucking leaves from trees.

ORNITHISCHIAN (BIRD-HIPPED) DINOSAURS

104 **You will be amazed to know that the Heterodontosaurus' hands were very well suited for grasping.** It had five fingers on each hand, of which two were opposable, which made holding things a little bit easier. It is also believed that the Heterodontosaurus had a fairly flexible tail, as it lacked any long, bony tail tendons. These tendons, while they helped the creature to stabilise itself, also stopped it from achieving a great degree of mobility.

105 **Scientists believe that the frightening tusks of the Heterodontosaurus could have been handy digging tools.** It might be a possibility that the Heterodontosaurus sifted through the topsoil with its blade like canines, scrounging for roots and other buried treasures. Perhaps these tusks were used to scare possible predators or to break into termite mounds.

106 **It is interesting to note that the offspring of the Heterodontosaurs had tusks too.** Palaeontologist Richard Butler, who worked on the specimen of a juvenile Heterodontosaurus skull identified in 2008, proudly displayed a pair of those iconic canines, disapproving the idea that tusks did not come about in the younger dinosaurs until after they reached maturity.

CERAPODA AND THYREOPHORA

107 **Can you believe that there existed polar dinosaurs just like polar bears?** They are called Leaellynasaura. These dinosaurs would have had to live without sunlight for several months of the year during the winters. They roamed Australia's southern tip around 110 million years ago.

108 **The Leaellynasaura had large and penetrating eyes.** They seem to have been blessed with a pair of unusually big eyeballs. This feature helped these dinosaurs to see better in the dark and avoid predators. There were enlarged optic lobes in their brain cavity, which indicate that they could process complex images in low light conditions.

109 **A very unusual and interesting fact about the Leaellynasaura is that its tail was unusually long and contained more than 70 vertebrae.** According to some recent estimates, the tail is made up around 75 per cent of its total body length. Till date, researchers are not sure about the use of this long tail.

ORNITHISCHIAN (BIRD-HIPPED) DINOSAURS

110 Earlier it was believed by scientists that the Leaellynasaura's metabolism annually slowed down as winter arrived, putting this dinosaur in a state of bear-like hibernation. Scientists based this idea on proofs of fluctuation in the growth rings in the fossilised bones that had been found. But now it is believed that unlike today's polar animals, Leaellynasaura probably did not hibernate.

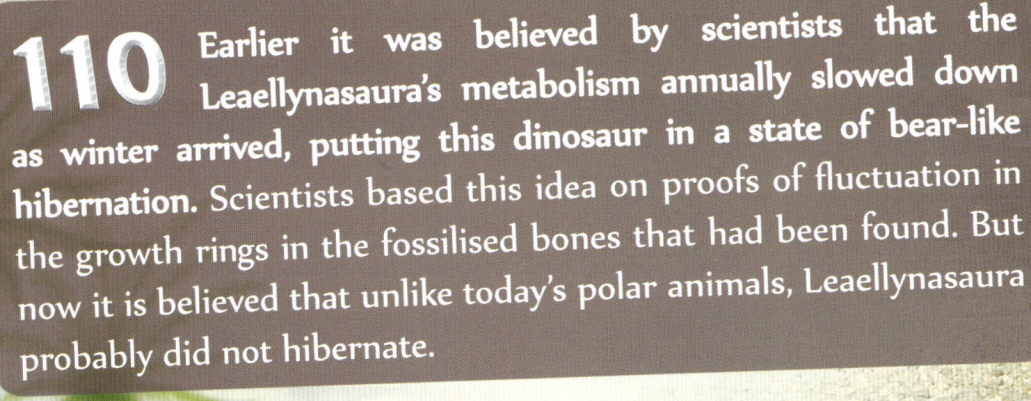

111 The upper and lower teeth of the Lesothosaurus were small and shaped like arrowheads. Some researchers think the Lesothosaurus was similar to a modern gazelle, grazing on low lying plants and running away quickly at the first sight of predators. It was named after Lesotho, the southern African country where its fossils were found in 1978.

112 Based on the study of specimens, scientists say there were many small ridges on the edges of the teeth of the Othnielosaurus which might have helped it shred the leaves. This dinosaur's vertebrae show that it had a small neck. The Othnielosaurus moved swiftly on its strong back limbs, which were built for running.

CERAPODA AND THYREOPHORA

113 Did you know that the Triceratops had around 400 to 800 teeth? Although it did not use all its teeth at one time. Instead, it used only a small percentage of these. The teeth of the Triceratops constantly got replaced throughout its lifetime. Out of its total length, the skull of a Triceratops alone could grow to more than two metres long.

114 The Triceratops is quite a popular creature. It is interesting to know that the US state of Wyoming lists the Triceratops as its official 'state dinosaur'. The popular 'Transformers' toy line and animated series also represented the Triceratops. In the animated series, an Autobot that could transform into a Triceratops was shown.

115 An interesting fact about the Stygimoloch is that some scientists believe that this dinosaur was actually a juvenile version of a Pachycephalosaurus. At present, this idea is not confirmed and is just a theory. It is believed that this dinosaur lived off a diet of horsetails, gingkos, cycads, seed ferns and club mosses.

ORNITHISCHIAN (BIRD-HIPPED) DINOSAURS

116 Did you know that the term 'Scelidosaurus' was coined by the same person who coined the word 'dinosaur'? In the year 1858, the first such specimen was discovered and after a year Sir Richard Owen termed this creature as the 'Scelidosaurus'. The name means 'limb lizard', and was chosen to represent its well-preserved hindquarters.

117 Scelidosaurus had scales which were small and bumpy. The skin impressions of its fossilised specimen revealed that Scelidosaurus, hide (at least the bits which were not covered in armoured plating) featured rounded and very tiny scales which created a pebbly, Gila monster-esque texture.

118 Though the Scelidosaurus was not a sea creature, all of its fossils have been found in rocks that were formed on the sea floor. This might be because it lived near the coast or perhaps a flood further inland killed a great number of these dinosaurs and washed them out to sea.

CERAPODA AND THYREOPHORA

119 The Scelidosaurus was named because of its armour or 'shield'. It seems to have been a slow mover, forced to walk on four legs rather than on two. It probably ate the low growing vegetation and is believed to have lived in the early Jurassic era.

120 In the year 2011, a very well-preserved skeleton cast was brought to be studied in the locally based dinosaur discovery site museum at Utah, sponsored by Virginius Dabney of St. George. Dabney donated almost all the necessary financial backing for this study on the request of his grandchildren.

121 Scientists found some bony plates on the skin of the Scelidosaurus, which were covered with tough keratin, the material your fingernails are made up of. These 'scutes' were as sharp as a knife's blade and would have helped to attack their enemies or predators.

ORNITHISCHIAN (BIRD-HIPPED) DINOSAURS

122 Large, diamond-shaped plates ran along the back of the Stegosaurus. Although the plates would have made Stegosaurus look bigger and more fearsome, they were not really any good as armour. The purpose of the plates is still uncertain; they may have been used for display or to help regulate body temperature.

123 Each shoulder of the Stegosaurs had a large spike, whereas pairs of smaller spikes lined the tail. It is believed by researchers that the spikes probably helped the dinosaur to ward off attackers. Each plate was covered with a tough, horn-like layer or skin.

CERAPODA AND THYREOPHORA

124 It was a common assumption that the plates found along the back of the Stegosaurus were part of its skeleton. On the contrary, these 17 plates arose from the skin, rather than being attached to the skeleton. It is also notable the largest plates were around 0.6 metres (two feet) tall and 0.6 metres wide.

125 Did you know that though the body of Stegosaurus was very large, the size of its brain was only about as big as the size of a dog's brain? The name of this dinosaur comes from the Greek word 'stegos' meaning 'roof' and 'sauros' meaning 'lizard'. They lived in the late Jurassic period around 150 million years ago.

126 Most dinosaurs had long hind legs and short fore legs. However, this was not the case with all Stegosaurs. One kind of Stegosaurs were the Huayangosaurus, which were exceptions in the family. Huayangosaurus had all four legs of almost the same length. The name of this dinosaur is derived from the place 'Huayang' where it was discovered.

ORNITHISCHIAN (BIRD-HIPPED) DINOSAURS

127 The Huayangosaurus is one of the early Stegosaurs which differed from later species in having a shorter, broader snout. It is believed that this dinosaur lived in the woodlands of the continents of Asia, particularly in China, around 165 million years ago in the middle of the Jurassic period.

128 One primitive feature in Huayangosaurus is that the skull had a small opening in front of each eye, and in each half of the lower jaw there was another small opening. These openings are not found in later Stegosaurs. The Huayangosaurus had 14 teeth (seven on each side) in front of its snout, which is another feature that disappeared in later Stegosaurs.

129 The Tuojiangosaurs had bony plates along its back and hips which were tall and triangular, whereas those on its neck were much smaller. Like other Stegosaurs, it had vicious spikes at the tip of its tail, allowing it to gore enemies or rivals with a violent lash of the tail.

CERAPODA AND THYREOPHORA

130 **Can you believe that the Kentrosaurus' brain was of the size of a walnut?** It is believed that the Kentrosaurus had a very small, but long brain. This dinosaur had a very good sense of smell, as the olfactory bulbs were well developed in the brain. Its name means 'sharp-point lizard'.

131 **It was believed for a long time by researchers that the Kentrosaurus had two brains—a tiny one in its head and a larger one in its rear end.** However it is now concluded by the researchers that its rear 'brain' was just an energy store and not a brain at all.

132 **Two rows of bony plates were embedded in the in the neck and back of Kentrosaurus.** There also existed two rows of spikes along its back and tail to fend off attacks from behind. It also had a pair of long spikes on the shoulders to protect itself from side attacks. A complete skull fossil has never been found, but it is believed that this dinosaur probably had a narrow snout and tiny teeth.

ORNITHISCHIAN (BIRD-HIPPED) DINOSAURS

133 **The Kentrosaurus could swing its tail spikes with skull cracking speed.** Dr. Heinrich Mallison of Tubingen University has calculated that the tail of this dinosaur could swing in a 180 degree arc, creating forces that could easily fracture a human skull.

134 **Remains of the Kentrosaurus, which are currently housed in Berlin, were scanned by a scientist named Mallison, who in the year 2005 created a digital prototype of the Kentrosaurus.** This helped in exploring the animal's range of motion. This digital Kentrosaurus also helped to study how flexible the neck of this dinosaur was, which probably helped it in spotting lurking predators.

CERAPODA AND THYREOPHORA

135 According to scientists, the thigh bones of the Kentrosaurus were of two kinds: robust and comparatively slender. It is assumed that fossils with thicker thighs were females, who formed harems around the less abundant males.

136 Did you know that even the eyelids of the Ankylosaurus were covered with small armour plates? The Ankylosaurus was the largest ever Ankylosaur, with hundreds of armour plates studding its thick skin. The armour was formed from bony plates called osteoderms that grew from the skin, much like the armour plating on a crocodile's skin.

137 The long tail of the Ankylosaurus ended in a huge and heavy club made up of solid bone. This massive tail club could be used by the dinosaur to generate a large amount of force, potentially breaking the bones of another dinosaur or other attackers while defending itself.

ORNITHISCHIAN (BIRD-HIPPED) DINOSAURS

138 Ankylosaurus in Greek means 'fused lizard' and this dinosaur got this name because the bones in its skull and other parts of its body were fused, making it extremely rugged. The Ankylosaurus lived about 66.5 million to 66.8 million years ago in the late Cretaceous period and roamed the western United States and Alberta, Canada.

139 Edmontonia, an Anlylosaur, seems to have been very dangerous as it had large spikes that pointed out from the sides of its body. The four of its largest spikes were located above the shoulders, and according to some scientists these spikes were for defense. It is also a possibility that larger and more developed spikes belong to more mature Edmontonia, just like in the case of deer antlers.

CERAPODA AND THYREOPHORA

141 Do you know the name of smallest Ankylosaur? One of the smallest Ankylosaur was Minmi. Small and rounded armour plates covered its body, including its belly. Extra bones along its back may have supported its back muscles. Its beak was sharp and it had small leaf-shaped teeth with saw-tooth edges.

142 The Gastonia was covered from head to tail with rows of huge blade-like spikes made of bone. This is why it is also sometimes called a walking fortress. Though the Gastonia is an Ankylosaur, it had no tail club. However, its spiked tail could swing from side to side to inflict savage injuries. The Gastonia weighed about a ton and measured around 15 feet in length.

140 The Edmontonia lived in an environment that changed throughout the year, with extended wet and dry periods. To make sure that their newly hatched young got a good supply of fresh vegetation, these dinosaurs would always lay eggs to hatch in time for the wet season.

ORNITHISCHIAN (BIRD-HIPPED) DINOSAURS

143 Scientists believe that only the bravest or most desperate predator would risk attacking the Gastonia. This is because the Gastonia weighed as much as a black rhino, ran at a speed of about eight miles per hour, and seemed to be a visibly dangerous animal with all its spikes. One of the few predators that would risk attacking it was the Utahraptor.

144 The had many unusual features for an Ankylosaur. Unlike other members of the family, it had teeth at the front of the upper jaw, and its armour plates were hollow. It also had straight nostrils instead of the odd, looping ones seen in other Ankylosaurs. It also had spikes on the sides of its body.

145 Predators might have risked deadly injuries if they tried to bite the Sauropelta's neck which bristled with horn-like spikes. The dinosaur looked much larger than it actually was, when viewed from the front, due to the rows of upward pointing spikes on its back. Scientists suggest that its spikes might have helped it deceive predators.

CERAPODA AND THYREOPHORA

146 **Do you know what Sauropelta means?** The meaning of Sauropelta is 'shield lizard'. It got this name because a thick shield of armour plates covered its back and tail. The shield was a jigsaw of small plates of bone that fitted together like tiles, giving this dinosaur an unusual look.

147 **One of the largest armoured dinosaurs (Ankylosaurs) was the Euoplocephalus.** It was twice the size of a rhinoceros and covered in heavy armour. Despite its stocky build and weight, it had powerful legs and may have been quite nimble on its feet.

ORNITHISCHIAN (BIRD-HIPPED) DINOSAURS

148 Like all Ankylosaurs, the Euoplocephalus had a tail club which it could swing at attackers. Its tail club, which is a terrifying feature, was supported by bony tendons. These tendons supported the tail, giving it the rigidity and strength of a hammer, along with the flexibility required to swing.

149 It is interesting to note that the Euoplocephalus's skull was covered with armour plates arranged like paving stones. There were even armoured shutters on its eyelids which slid down to protect the eyes of this dinosaur. It also had stout, massive arm bones to support its heavy body.

150 The Euoplocephalus seems to have been a unique masticator dinosaur. Generally, dinosaurs swallowed their food whole, or mashed it by slamming their teeth together in a straight vertical motion. But the Euoplocephalus could tear apart vegetation with ease by moving its lower jaw backwards.

CERAPODA AND THYREOPHORA

151 Based on fossil remains, scientists believe that the Euoplocephalus had very strong neck armour. A cervical half ring is found in its neck. This ring was formed by fusing together of several bony plates in an arch-shaped block that was draped over this dinosaurs neck.

152 At the start of the Triassic period, all dinosaurs were small and stood low on the ground. Over time, a group of mainly plant-eating dinosaurs called Prosauropods grew taller and heavier than their competitors. They evolved long necks and tails and strong back legs that allowed them to stand up and reach high tree branches.

153 As the name suggests 'Prosauropods' means 'before the Sauropods', and it is believed that this group of dinosaurs were the ancestors of the Sauropoda. Prosauropods had sharp teeth that could slice through tough leaf stems. They also had a long, curved thumb claw for defence and for grasping tree branches.

ORNITHISCHIAN (BIRD-HIPPED) DINOSAURS

154 Could you imagine a dinosaur standing like a kangaroo? It is hard to imagine, but there existed a dinosaur, in the late Triassic era around 220–210 million years ago, which could stand like a kangaroo. The Plateosaurus could stand like a kangaroo, rearing up on its hind limbs and stretching its long neck to eat leaves from trees.

155 Scientists have found fossils that suggest that a few adult Plateosauri suffered from stunted or confounded growth. Generally an adult Plateosaurus' length ranged from 4.5 to 10 metres but it seems that some of these Plateosauri reached less than half the size of an adult or in other words, it is suggested that some of them were dwarves.

156 The Plateosaurus had plenty of room for supersized lungs, as it had flexible ribs arranged in a large, barrel-shaped cage. This might have helped the Plateosaurus to take deep breaths, which would have been useful for them as the Earth's atmosphere contained significantly less oxygen than it does today.

CERAPODA AND THYREOPHORA

157 The teeth of the Massospondylus suggest that it could chew both meat and plants. This dinosaur is noted for having two kinds of teeth: small pointed teeth in the anterior part of the mouth similar to those of Theropods, and spatulate teeth in the posterior of the mouth.

158 The Massospondylus had five fingered hands, which it used to grasp and pull down branches. It may have also used its long thumb claws to tear off pieces of plant material. The Massospondylus used its long tail to maintain its balance.

159 Scientists believe that the Massospondylus may have swallowed small stones to help digest its food, because they found stomach stones among the bones of the Massospondylus. This dinosaur lived in the woodlands of South Africa around 200–183 million years ago, in the early Jurassic era.

ORNITHISCHIAN (BIRD-HIPPED) DINOSAURS

160 Researchers found that there were large blood vessels present in the cheeks of the Massospondylus, which most likely supplied oxygenated blood to the cheeks of this dinosaur. The cheeks would have prevented food from falling out while it was being processed by the teeth, which also suggests that they were largely herbivorous creatures.

161 The Thecodontosaurus was the first Prosauropod to be discovered. It was named 'socket toothed' after its unusual leaf shaped, saw-like teeth. Unlike today's lizards, whose teeth are fused to their jaw bones, this Prosauropod's teeth were rooted in a separate socket in its jaw.

CERAPODA AND THYREOPHORA

162 It is believed by palaeontologists that since Thecodontosaurus were smaller in size as compared to their relatives, they may have lived on islands. This is because animals that live on islands are often small in size. Many fossils of Thecodontosaurus have been found in caves, and may have been washed there by rising sea levels.

163 The Lufengosaurus was the first dinosaur to be mounted and assembled for display in China. It is one of the most popular exhibits in Chinese natural history displays concerning dinosaurs. Lufengosaurus L. Huenei was the first species of the Lufengosaurus to be discovered, and was named in 1940.

ORNITHISCHIAN (BIRD-HIPPED) DINOSAURS

164 The Lufengosaurus had teeth which were blade like and whose crowns were wider at the bottom. It used its sharp teeth to eat tough plants or to nibble on leaves from trees. It may also have eaten small animals occassionaly though it is thought that this dinosaur probably ate only plants.

165 Did you know that even scientists face a lot of confusion about classifying fossilised remains? For instance, according to many palaeontologists, the Lufengosaurus had a confusing relationship with the genus Gyposaurus. Peter Galton considered the species G. Sinensis to be a juvenile of Lufengosaurus in the year 1976. However, a particular species of Gyposaurus, G. Capensis, had already been popularly associated with the Massospondylus.

CERAPODA AND THYREOPHORA

166 **The Ammosaurus is considered a versatile animal, which was able to move both bipedally and quadrupdally and may have been omnivorous.** The name of this dinosaur is derived from the Greek word 'ammos' which means 'sandy ground'. The weight of the Ammosaurus was estimated to be around 70 kilograms by Gregory S. Paul in the year 2010.

167 **The first discovery of Anchisaurus remains was made much before the world knew anything about dinosaurs.** These fossils were discovered in North America, and thus it was the first dinosaur discovery there. Here, some large bones were discovered in Connecticut, USA in the year 1818.

ORNITHISCHIAN (BIRD-HIPPED) DINOSAURS

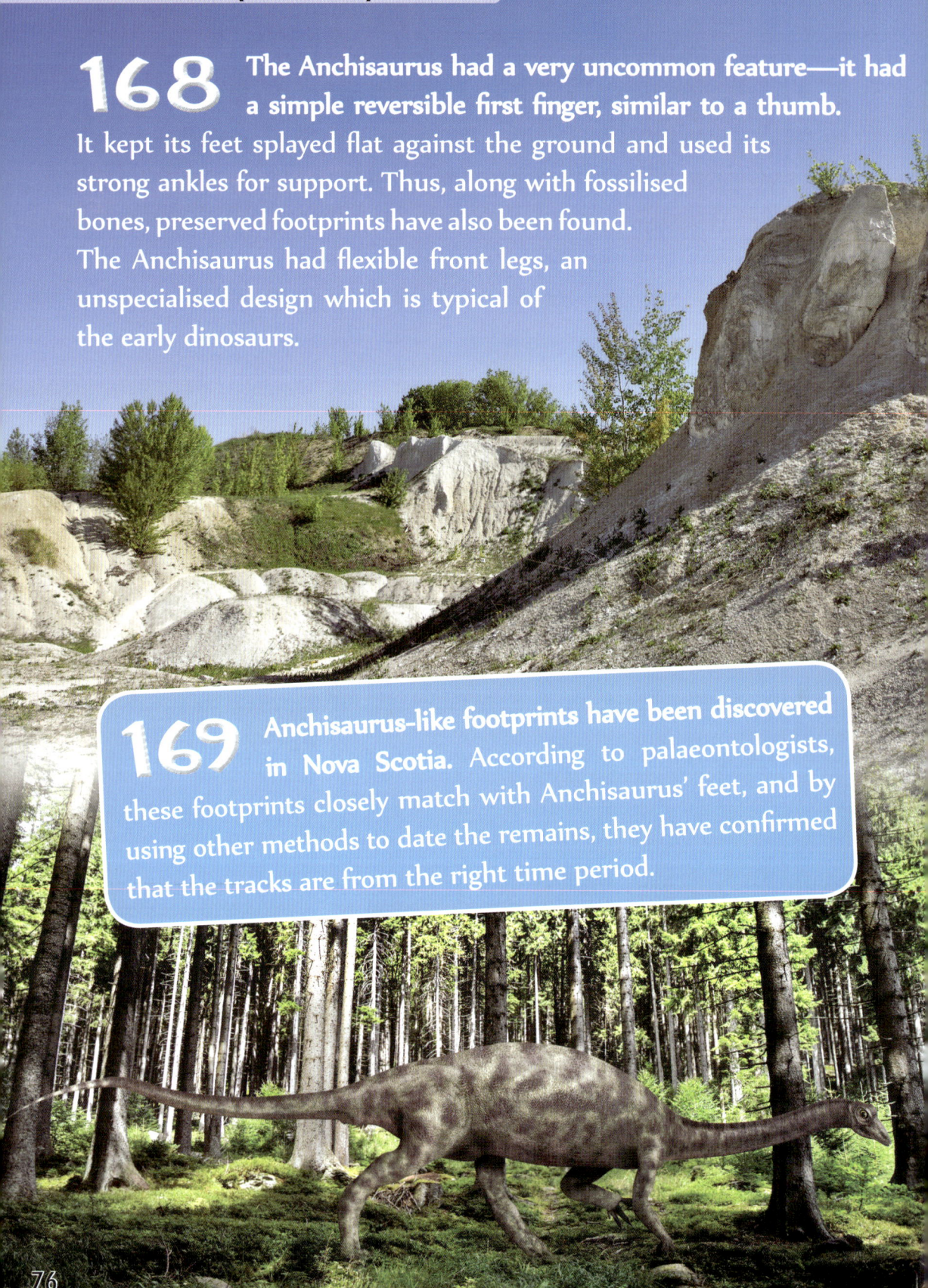

168 The Anchisaurus had a very uncommon feature—it had a simple reversible first finger, similar to a thumb. It kept its feet splayed flat against the ground and used its strong ankles for support. Thus, along with fossilised bones, preserved footprints have also been found. The Anchisaurus had flexible front legs, an unspecialised design which is typical of the early dinosaurs.

169 Anchisaurus-like footprints have been discovered in Nova Scotia. According to palaeontologists, these footprints closely match with Anchisaurus' feet, and by using other methods to date the remains, they have confirmed that the tracks are from the right time period.

CERAPODA AND THYREOPHORA

170 It is amazing that despite being a primitive Sauropodomorph or 'long-necked' dinosaur, the Anchisaurus did share certain anatomical traits with later members of the group. For instance, the hands of this dinosaur were proportionally short, relative to the arm as a whole.

171 Did you know, the Anchisaurus had to be re-named twice in order to get its proper name? In 1865, geologist Edward Hitchcock had dubbed this dinosaur 'Megadactylus', but unfortunately it was found that another animal had already been given that name. It was then re-named as 'Amphisaurus', before finally being called 'Anchisaurus'.

ORNITHISCHIAN (BIRD-HIPPED) DINOSAURS

172 **The Riojasaurus was a cathemeral dinosaur.** 'Cathemeral' dinosaur means that it was active for short periods during both the day and night. Scientists know this from the sclera rings of the eyes in the fossil remains. The Riojasaurus had its rear limbs slightly longer than the fore limbs, but this was not a very large difference.

173 **On 3 December, 2004, the scientific community declared that the Unaysaurus, discovered in Southern Brazil in 1998, was one of the oldest dinosaurs.** The Unaysaurus was a member of the plant-eating dinosaurs group known as Prosauropods. It was relatively small and walked on two legs like most early dinosaurs.

CERAPODA AND THYREOPHORA

174 The Lexovisaurus was first named the Omosauruswas. However, it was later realised that the name Omosauruswas had already been given to another fossil. The fossil of this dinosaur was then renamed as Dacentrutus in 1915, and then finally in the year 1957 a French palaeontologist named this fossil as a new genus, Lexovisaurus.

175 The Tatisaurus is counted as a dubious dinosaur. This is because of the severe lack of fossils for this dinosaur. Despite the limited evidence, palaeontologists prefer to label the Tatisaurus as a probably primitive Thyreophoran dinosaur.

ORNITHISCHIAN (BIRD-HIPPED) DINOSAURS

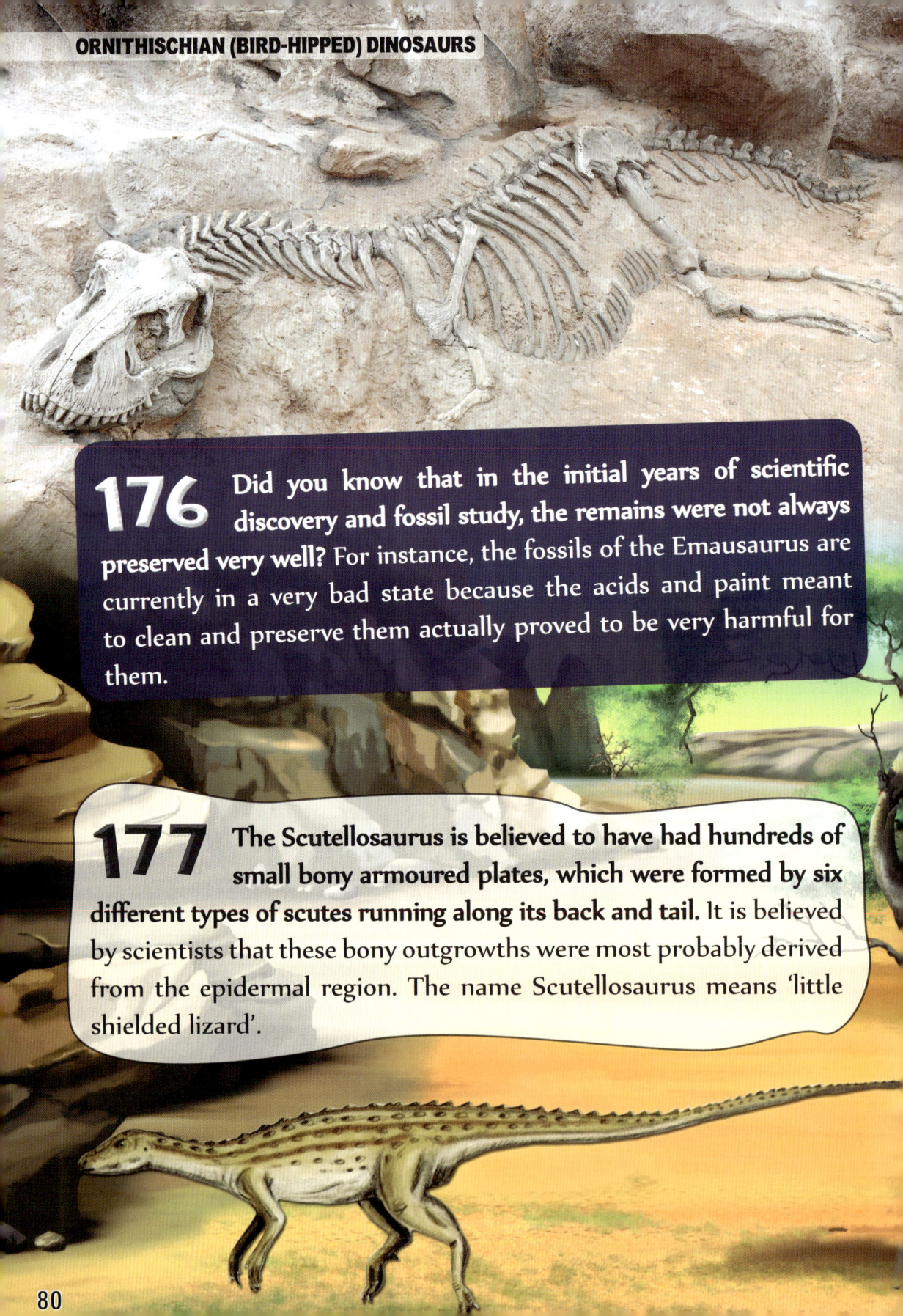

176 Did you know that in the initial years of scientific discovery and fossil study, the remains were not always preserved very well? For instance, the fossils of the Emausaurus are currently in a very bad state because the acids and paint meant to clean and preserve them actually proved to be very harmful for them.

177 The Scutellosaurus is believed to have had hundreds of small bony armoured plates, which were formed by six different types of scutes running along its back and tail. It is believed by scientists that these bony outgrowths were most probably derived from the epidermal region. The name Scutellosaurus means 'little shielded lizard'.

CERAPODA AND THYREOPHORA

178 An anatomical study of the skull of the Scutellosaurus showed that they did not have any cheeks! It is presumed that this dinosaur swallowed its food as a whole, without chewing its food. They do have teeth shaped like a leaf, which helped them snap off vegetation that they ate.

179 The Lusitanosaurus is represented by a fossil which includes a single partial left maxilla and an upper jaw bone with seven teeth. According to scientists, the species was common in the region of Portugal. Because of the limited fossil remains, there is no way to determine the size of the Lusitanosaurus, but it can be inferred from the remains of its teeth and jaw, that it was herbivorous.

180 One of the first armoured dinosaurs known to have lived in Antarctica was the Antarctopelta. We must remember that during the time when the Antarctopelta lived in Antarctica, it was not covered in snow and ice. Thus, the climatic conditions were completely different.

SAURISCHIAN (LIZARD-HIPPED) DINOSAURS

Sauropoda

181 You will be amazed to know that the largest animal to ever live on land belongs to the Sauropoda group. This group is notable for the enormous sizes attained by some of its members. Sauropoda had small heads as compared to the rest of their body and very long necks and tails.

182 The name 'Sauropoda' was coined by O.C. Marsh, in the year 1878. It is derived from a Greek word which means 'lizard foot'. Sauropods are one of the most widespread and recognisable dinosaur groups. They have become known figures in popular culture due to their large sizes.

SAUROPODA

183 Did you know that even a dwarf Sauropod dinosaur was about six metres in length and could be counted among the largest animals in their ecosystem? A dwarf Sauropod was approximately the size of a blue whale. It can be said that the most defining characteristic of Sauropods was their size.

184 When Sauropods were first discovered, most scientists compared them with modern day whales. Most scientists believe that due to their immense weight, Sauropods could not have supported their weight on land. This implies that they must have been mainly aquatic. Through the first three quarters of the 20th century, most representations of Sauropods portrayed them fully or partially immersed in water.

SAURISCHIAN (LIZARD-HIPPED) DINOSAURS

185 **Scientists believe that Sauropods consumed as much grass as they did leaves.** Scientists also concluded that the necks of Sauropods primarily swung from side to side and the great length of these dinosaurs enabled them to graze over huge areas of ground, without having to move their large bodies.

186 **It is hard to believe that the Brachiosaurus weighed between 30–50 tonnes-nearly a dozen times heavier than an African elephant.** It was one of the largest Sauropods. This unusual dinosaur lived around 156–150 million years ago, during the mid to late Jurassic period. It is believed to have been a warm-blooded animal.

187 **Have you ever wondered how much food a dinosaur could eat?** The Brachiosaurus, for instance, ate about 200 kg of leaves and twigs a day! This dinosaur used its spoon-shaped teeth to snip leaves from the tops of conifers, tree ferns and other trees.

SAUROPODA

188

The Brachiosaurus' forelimbs were longer compared to their hind limbs. The name of this dinosaur is also based on this fact and is a combination of the Greek word 'brakhion' and 'saurus'— meaning 'arm lizard'. It walked on all four legs. Compared to other Sauropods, the Brachiosaurus had a relatively shorter tail.

189

It is an interesting fact that the skull of the Brachiosaurus could be easily detached from its neck. Scientists believe that the tiny-brained skulls of the Brachiosaurus were only loosely attached to the rest of their skeletons and thus were easily detached after their deaths, either by predators or by natural erosion.

SAURISCHIAN (LIZARD-HIPPED) DINOSAURS

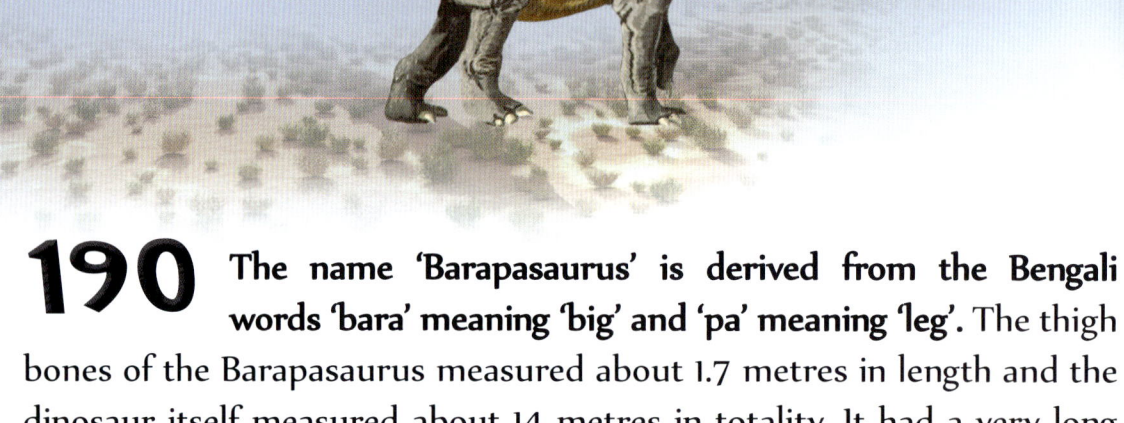

190 The name 'Barapasaurus' is derived from the Bengali words 'bara' meaning 'big' and 'pa' meaning 'leg'. The thigh bones of the Barapasaurus measured about 1.7 metres in length and the dinosaur itself measured about 14 metres in totality. It had a very long neck. You can imagine this dinosaur to be two to three times larger than a grown elephant.

191 It is interesting to note that unlike other Sauropods, the Barapasaurus had sharp teeth with saw-like edges. In terms of size, the largest known tooth of Barapasaurus is about 0.058 metres. In order to gather leaves from the trees, it used its teeth like a rake; and as it was not able to chew, it simply swallowed everything that came between its teeth.

SAUROPODA

192 **The Mamenchisaurus had one of the longest necks of any known animal.** The neck of the Mamenchisaurus was supported by 19 long bones. This Sauropod's neck moved freely from side to side and made it easier for it to reach around itself.

193 **The Mamenchisaurus sinocanadorum, a variety of the Mamenchisaurus, is considered to be Asia's largest dinosaur.** Scientists are still not sure which was the world's the biggest dinosaur to exist as newer discoveries keep modifying our knowledge. However, the Mamenchisaurus sinocanadorum, which is estimated to be around 35.052 metres (115 foot) in length, clearly deserves to be a contender for the top spot.

194 **Another member of the Mamenchisaurus family was the Mamenchisaurus youngi which might have had to hold its tail permanently at an upturned and awkward 20 degree angle.** The vertebrae above its hips were fused together in a strange, V-shaped orientation, which was the reason behind its awkward tail posture.

SAURISCHIAN (LIZARD-HIPPED) DINOSAURS

195 **The Vulcanodon was so named because its first fossils were found in rocks near volcanoes.** Like other Sauropods, the Vulcanodon moved slowly on land. Its stubby, pillar-like limbs were useful in supporting its heavy body, but were not meant for running. It lived in the region now known as Zimbabwe, in the early Jurassic period.

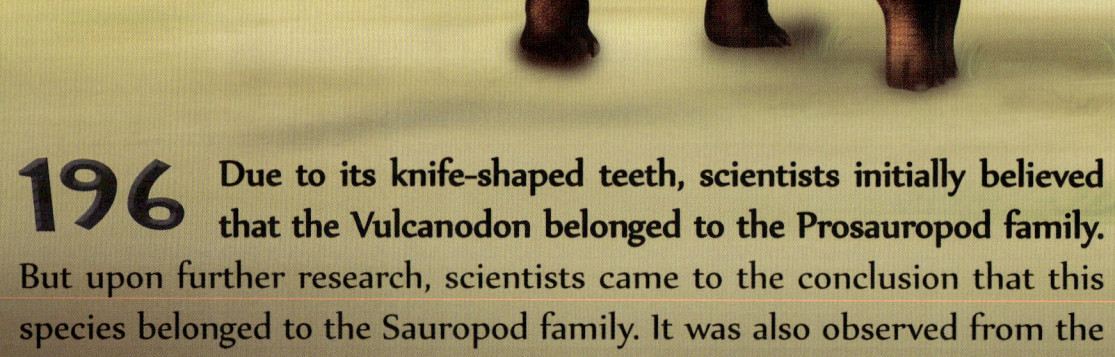

196 **Due to its knife-shaped teeth, scientists initially believed that the Vulcanodon belonged to the Prosauropod family.** But upon further research, scientists came to the conclusion that this species belonged to the Sauropod family. It was also observed from the identified fossil specimens that this dinosaur was about 6.5 metres long.

197 **Column-like legs, a long neck and tail are unique distinguishing characteristics of the Vulcanodon.** Scientists have been able to suggest what the Vulcanodon was like, based on their study of its fragmentary skeleton, including much of the pelvic girdle, hind limbs, forearms and tail. However, the fossils did not include the trunk, neck vertebrae, and the skull.

SAUROPODA

198 An amazing fact about the Camarasaurus is that it had a small, box-shaped head with a blunt snout and huge nostrils. Its long tail served to counterbalance its long neck. This creature had thick legs; its front legs were slightly shorter than its hind legs and its rear surface was only slightly sloped.

199 The spine of Camarasaurus had many hollow chambers. It is believed that these bones were connected to air sacks. This feature would have helped the creature breathe more efficiently. These chambers also helped reduce body weight and gave the Camarasaurus its name, which means 'chambered lizard'.

200 You will be amazed to learn that the worn-out teeth of the Camarasaurus were replaced with new ones every 62 days. The shape and size of its teeth suggests that food was at least partially processed before swallowing. They had very strong jaws filled with large chiselled teeth designed for chopping tough and coarse plants.

SAURISCHIAN (LIZARD-HIPPED) DINOSAURS

201 Scientists believe that the Camarasaurus did not lay eggs in well-built nests, unlike many other Sauropods. Female Camarasuarus probably laid eggs while they walked and did not show parental care. It is also believed that Camarasaurus were able to reproduce at the age of 20 years.

202 Palaeontologists assume that the Camarasaurus was a social creature, because fossils of both adult and young dinosaurs were often found close to each other. They lived and travelled in herds. The Camarasaurus lived in the region now known as North America, in the late Jurassic period, around 155–145 million years ago.

SAUROPODA

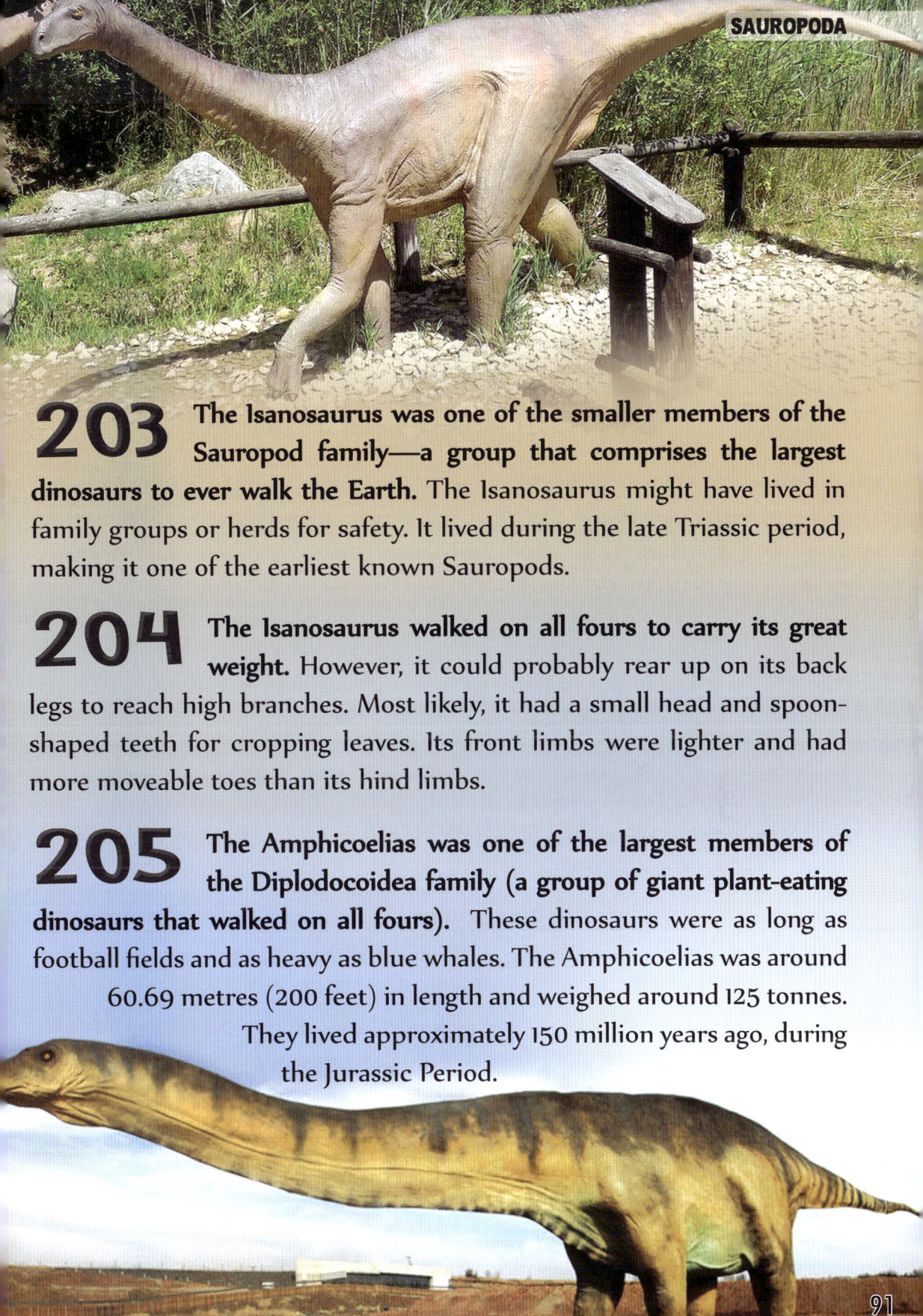

203 **The Isanosaurus was one of the smaller members of the Sauropod family—a group that comprises the largest dinosaurs to ever walk the Earth.** The Isanosaurus might have lived in family groups or herds for safety. It lived during the late Triassic period, making it one of the earliest known Sauropods.

204 **The Isanosaurus walked on all fours to carry its great weight.** However, it could probably rear up on its back legs to reach high branches. Most likely, it had a small head and spoon-shaped teeth for cropping leaves. Its front limbs were lighter and had more moveable toes than its hind limbs.

205 **The Amphicoelias was one of the largest members of the Diplodocoidea family (a group of giant plant-eating dinosaurs that walked on all fours).** These dinosaurs were as long as football fields and as heavy as blue whales. The Amphicoelias was around 60.69 metres (200 feet) in length and weighed around 125 tonnes. They lived approximately 150 million years ago, during the Jurassic Period.

SAURISCHIAN (LIZARD-HIPPED) DINOSAURS

206 Some controversy surrounds the Amphioelias; a few palaeontologists believe this species did not actually exist. The backbone fossil specimens upon which palaeontologist Edward Drinker Cope based his findings no longer exist. It is possible that he may have made a clerical error as he tried to keep up with the frantic pace of the discovery, which was common during the 'Bone Wars' of the 19th century—the popular name given to the rivalry between E.D. Cope and another palaeontologist, Othniel Charles Marsh.

207 The Dicraeosaurus had a shorter neck and a larger head than other Diplodocoids. Its neck contained 12 short vertebrae, so it could probably browse vegetation only at the ground level, up to a height of three metres. Its tail was also shorter which suggests it was not used like a whip for defence.

208 A layer of skin may have stretched between the bony spines that ran along the neck and back of the Dicraeosaurus, forming a sail. This might have helped to regulate its body temperature, or may have been used for defence or for communicating with other members of the species.

SAUROPODA

The backbone of a Diplodocus acted like the cables in a suspension bridge.

209 It is interesting that to support the long neck and tail of the Diplodocus, its backbone acted like the cables in a suspension bridge. Just as the cables take the weight of the bridge and pass it down through the piers which anchor it to the ground, the backbone took the weight of the neck and tail, and passed it through to the legs and onto the ground.

210 Scientists have found the fossils of many dinosaurs, but most of them are fragmentary, and missing one or the other part. The Diplodocus is one of the few dinosaurs of which a complete skeleton fossil has been found. It reached lengths of about 30 metres, and had a unique body construction, with spines running along its neck, back and tail to provide extra support and superior mobility. Its name is derived from the Greek words 'diplos' meaning 'double' and 'dokos' meaning 'beam'.

211 The Diplodocus had an incredibly long tail—as long as the rest of its body—which it could move at an amazing speed, creating a whip-like effect. It is believed that it carried its tail off the ground, at a roughly horizontal level. The purpose of the whip-like end is still not clear.

SAURISCHIAN (LIZARD-HIPPED) DINOSAURS

212 **A really amazing fact about the Diplodocus is that its neck was almost three times the length of a giraffe's neck and was probably held up at a high angle.** Scientists believe that the Diplodocus held its neck at a 45-degree angle most of the time. Its neck and tail made up the majority of its length.

213 **Diplodocus may have grown at a very high rate, taking just around 10 years to become full-sized adults.** As compared to the size of its body, it had a very small head and would have had a very small brain. Its backbone was strong enough to support its enormous weight, but the bones were hollow.

214 **Amargasaurus were relatively small and short-necked Diplodocoids.** They were unusual as they had a double row of spines running along the neck and back, that became a single line down its tail. Among the two rows of spikes, the largest were placed along the neck.

SAUROPODA

215 **The purpose of the Amargasaurus' spinal structure is a mystery.** There may have been a web of skin running between the spines, forming a double sail, which might have been used for display by them. Some scientists think these dinosaurs did not have a sail and simply rattled the spines to make noise, scaring predators away.

216 **The Apatosaurus had another name: Brontosaurus.** When Othniel Charles Marsh first discovered the bones of a giant dinosaur, he named this dinosaur Apatosaurus (meaning 'deceptive lizard'). Later, he found some larger bones and thought they were of a different species and named it Brontosaurus (meaning 'thunder lizard'). Finally, it came to be known that both sets of bones were of the same kind of dinosaur.

217 **The Apatosaurus weighed as much as four elephants and was shorter and heavier than its relatives.** It had thicker legs than those of its relatives as well. Some scientists think that instead of rearing up to feed from trees, Apatosaurus may have used its strong limbs and massive weight to knock trees down. Pencil-like teeth lined the front of its broad muzzle.

SAURISCHIAN (LIZARD-HIPPED) DINOSAURS

218 Scientists believe that the Barosaurus swallowed stones to help grind food in its stomach, as its large peg-like teeth were perfect for pulling the leaves off trees, but not for chewing them. However, recent research has suggested that they used bacteria present in their gut to digest food.

219 In 1993, a model Barosaurus was mounted rearing upon its hind legs. Some scientists think this position is incorrect as its heart could not have been strong enough to pump blood up to the brain. On the other hand, others have suggested that it might have had more than one heart or a larger-sized heart than was earlier believed.

220 The rough, scaly skin of the Barosaurus gave it much-needed protection against scratches and bite wounds. It also helped reduce moisture loss from its body when the climate turned dry. These spines were bony plates fixed in the skin and were not attached to the skeleton.

SAUROPODA

221 You will be amazed to know that the neck of the Barosaurus was around 9.5 metres (30 feet) in length, which allowed it to reach leaves at the tops of trees. This feature was an advantage over other plant-eating dinosaurs. Barosaurus was heavier than three elephants and longer than a tennis court. It had all the usual features of Sauropods: a bulky body, a tiny head and relatively short legs.

222 The Barosaurus was very similar to the Diplodocus, but there existed slight differences: the Barasaurus had much longer backbones, a much longer neck and a shorter tail. However, just like the Diplodocus, Barosaurus also had 15 cervical vertebrae, out of which some were more than one metre long. The neck as a whole was probably light, due to scoops and hollows in their arrangements.

223 Scientists believe that the Barosaurus used its long tail to protect itself from attackers. It swung its tail or stomped the attacking dinosaur, and in order to do this the Barosaurus dinosaur had to stand up on its hind legs. In this position, it was so tall, it could have looked over the top of a five-storey building!

SAURISCHIAN (LIZARD-HIPPED) DINOSAURS

224 Titanosaurs were among the heaviest animals ever to walk on the Earth. They were also among the last of the dinosaurs. Named after the Titans (a race of giants in Greek mythology), these dinosaurs were plant eaters and probably lived in herds to protect themselves against predators or attackers.

225 The skull of the Nemegtosaurus had sclera ring-like structures, mostly found in reptiles. It also had a bony support for the eye. Scientists believe that the Nemegtosaurus was active for short periods of time throughout the day. It lived around 80–60 million years ago in the woodlands of Asia.

226 The discovery of thousands of eggs of Titanosaurs scattered across a vast area in Argentina suggests that they nested together, in groups. It is estimated that Titanosaurs grew up to nine–12 metres in length and weighed about 13 tonnes. It is also believed that this dinosaur lived in the Cretaceous period in regions that now fall in India.

SAUROPODA

227 The Nemegtosaurus was named after the Nemegt Basin area in the Gobi desert of Mongolia, where it was first discovered. It is believed that it may have had a sloping head and small, peg-shaped teeth at the front of its jaws. Its neck was probably long and flexible, allowing it to feed on high tree branches.

228 Did you know that the size of an egg of the Argentinosaurus was about the size of a rugby ball? Scientists believe that it probably took around 40 years for a young one to reach adult size. Despite its massive size, it was hunted by Mapusaurus, a giant flesh eating dinosaur.

229 The Argentinosaurus was one of the largest and heaviest land animals. Scientists believe that the Argentinosaurus was longer than a tennis court and nearly 20 times heavier than an elephant. It also had elephant-like thick limbs and clawed toes. It weighed somewhere between 75–100 tonnes.

SAURISCHIAN (LIZARD-HIPPED) DINOSAURS

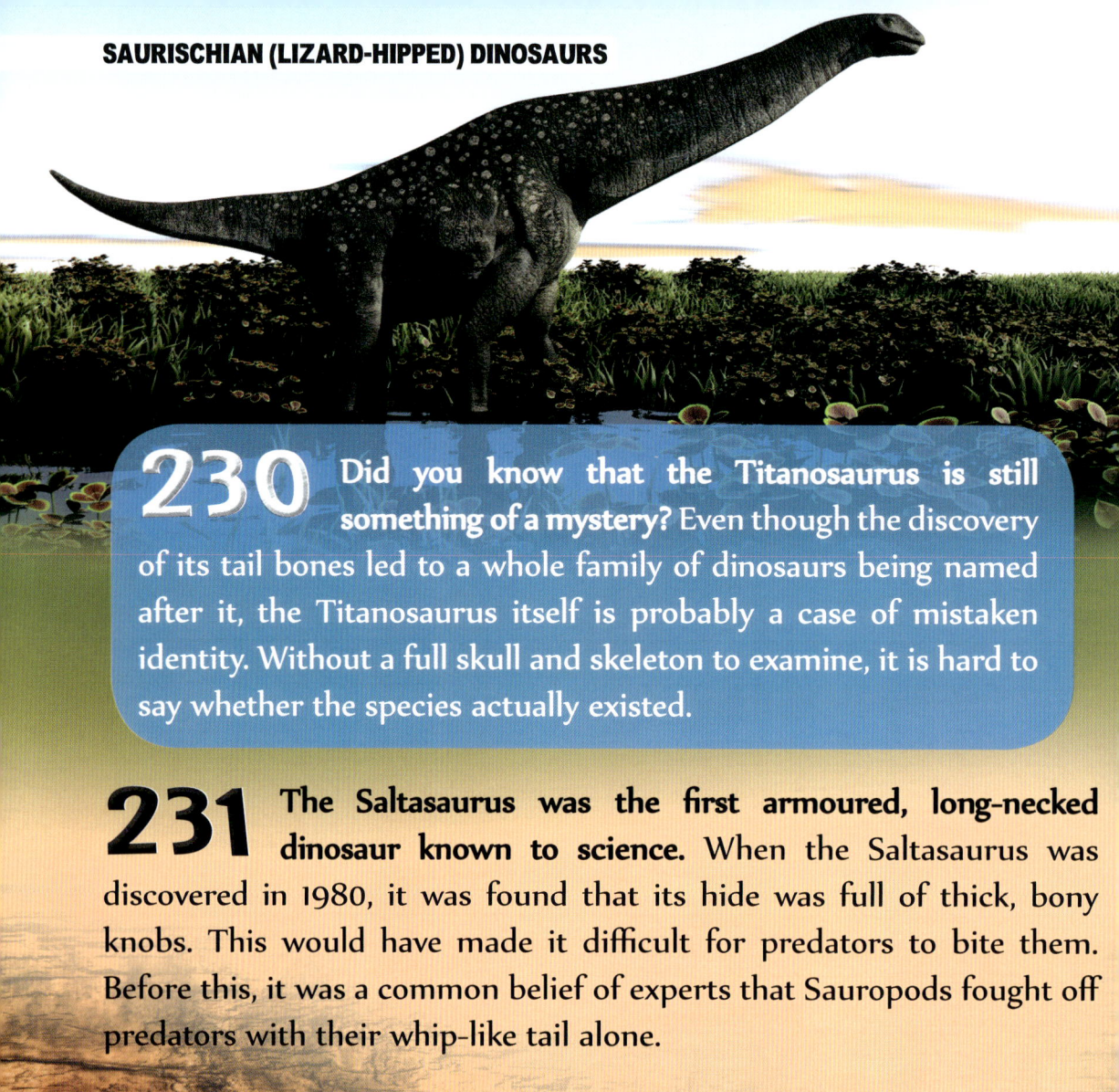

230 **Did you know that the Titanosaurus is still something of a mystery?** Even though the discovery of its tail bones led to a whole family of dinosaurs being named after it, the Titanosaurus itself is probably a case of mistaken identity. Without a full skull and skeleton to examine, it is hard to say whether the species actually existed.

231 **The Saltasaurus was the first armoured, long-necked dinosaur known to science.** When the Saltasaurus was discovered in 1980, it was found that its hide was full of thick, bony knobs. This would have made it difficult for predators to bite them. Before this, it was a common belief of experts that Sauropods fought off predators with their whip-like tail alone.

232 **The Saltasaurus was a relatively small Titanosaur, but was well protected against attacks.** Large predators could not rip open its thick armoured hide, which had plates and studs made of bone. Its strong hips and wide upper-tail bones suggest that it may have been able to stand on its hind legs, using its tail to prop itself up.

SAUROPODA

233 Isolated bones of the Saltasaurus were mistaken for pieces of a very different creature. In the 1920s, Freidrich von Huene located some samples of what has now been established as Saltasaurus armour. At that time, armour-plated Sauropods were not known. Therefore, he suggested that these might have come from a tank-like creature called the Loricosaurus—an armoured Ankylosaur.

234 The Isisaurus differed from other Titanosaurs because it stood more like a hyena, with the help of its long front legs and shorter neck. Its fossilised dung contained fungi found on many types of leaves. This suggests that it sampled leaves from different trees.

235 In the year 1994, a species of Titanosaurs, known as 'Phuwiangosaurus' was first named. It was the first named Sauropod dinosaur known to have come from Thailand. Scientists have only managed to piece together about 10 per cent of its skeleton, and many questions about its existence are still unanswered.

SAURISCHIAN (LIZARD-HIPPED) DINOSAURS

236 The Opisthocoelicaudia is named after its tail structure and means 'rear cavity tail'. An unusual feature about it is that the vertebrae of its tail curved deeply inward (it was concave) from the side that faced the end of the tail. The side that faced the front of the vertebrae of the animal was deeply curved outward (it was convex).

237 Scientists believe that the Opisthocoelicaudia may have used its tail as a prop, like the third leg of a tripod, in order to reach up to higher plants and trees. It might have helped this dinosaur take some of its weight off its back legs and provide proper balance.

238 The new hatchlings that came out of the soccer-ball sized eggs of the Rapetosaurus, which lived on the island of Madagascar, were of adult size. The newborn hatchlings seem to have been fully functioning and did not need parental support. It is believed that they would actively forage for plants themselves, instead of waiting for their mothers to feed them.

SAUROPODA

239 The Melanorosaurus was about 0.2286 metres (nine inches) in length and had a somewhat triangular skull that was full of openings to reduce the overall skull weight. Its jawbone was fused with 38 teeth (each side had 19 teeth) and its nose resembled a bird's beak due to a tapering and pointed structure.

240 The thumb or 'pollex' was twisted and shortened in the Antetonitrus for grasping things against the hand. They could easily lock their hand by arranging their large and thick wrist bones into a permanent pronated position for full-time weight support. This dinosaur also showed adaptability for an increased body size, which was seen in the later Sauropods.

241 An interesting feature of the Spinophorosaurus is that at the end of its tail it had a fierce set of spikes arranged in a fashion similar to the thagomizer arrangement found in some Stegosaurid dinosaurs. It also had two pairs of large, bony spikes near the end of its tail. Spinophorosaurus means 'spine bearing lizard' and it is believed that it lived in the middle of the Jurassic era.

SAURISCHIAN (LIZARD-HIPPED) DINOSAURS

242 Despite being a Sauropod, the Shunosaurus had very short neck. It did have a club-like formation at the end of its tail, like many Sauropods, but its tail club was also equipped with two successive spikes formed by a five centimetre (1.96 metres) long cone-shaped osteoderms. Its name is derived from 'Shu' which is an ancient name for the Sichuan province in China.

243 It is really amazing to learn that palaeontologists in China have identified five different species of the Omeisaurus. All these species of Omeisaurus are named after the locations where they were discovered. The species include O. junghsiensis, O. changshouensis, O. luoquanensis, O. tianfuensis, and O. fuxiensis. The Omeisaurus was named after the sacred mountain, Mount Omeishan.

244 The Cetiosaurus had solid vertebrae which hint that it was quite low on the level of evolution among Sauropods. Its name is derived from the Greek word 'keteios' which means 'sea monster'. Sir Richard Owen thought the Cetiosaurus was a marine creature like a huge crocodile, and did not recognise it for a land-dwelling dinosaur.

SAUROPODA

245 Generally, Saurapods like the Diplodocus and Apatosaurus had complicated vertebrae and whip-like tails. Comparatively, Jobaria (a primitive Sauropod) had a simple backbone and tail structure. The weight distribution of Jobaria suggests that it was supported by its rear limbs rather than its forelimbs. According to palaeontologist Paul Sereno, it may also have been able to rear up on its hind legs.

246 Did you know that most of the bones from the fossils of the Kaatedocus were lost in a fire at the American Museum of Natural History during the 1940s? Others had started rotting because they had been stowed in a chicken run at Shell (in Wyoming, USA) and had to be thrown away. Only about 10 per cent of the total fossils survived!

Theropoda

247 Scientists believe that Theropods were the world's top predators throughout the dinosaur age. This branch of the dinosaur family tree gave rise to some truly gigantic carnivores, though not all Theropods were meat eaters. Theropods flourished from the late Triassic to the late Cretaceous era.

248 Did you know that some scientists believe that one particular group of Theropods, known as Coelurosauria, evolved into the birds that share our world today, and are thus represented by 10,000 living species? Many of the Theropods had a furcula, or wishbone, and birds today have this feature as well.

249 The Giganotosaurus was a formidable predator and weighed as much as the combined weight of 125 human beings. This dinosaur is considered to be one of the largest meat-eating dinosaurs. It belongs to the Carcharodontosauridae ('shark-toothed lizards') family and was more than capable of preying on the giant Sauropods that roamed in present-day South America during the late Cretaceous period.

250 A common error people make is that often Giganotosaurus is mistranslated or mispronounced as 'Gigantosaurus' and people think it means 'gigantic lizard'. But the name Giganotosaurus is derived from the Greek terms 'gigas' meaning 'giant', 'notos' meaning 'south' and 'sauros' meaning 'lizard'—'giant southern lizard'.

251 Even though the Giganotosaurus was of a very big size and faster than the Tyrannosaurus Rex, it had an unusually small brain for its size. Scientists also say that its tiny brain appears to have been approximately the shape and weight of a banana.

252 Palaeontologists believe that the Giganotosaurus may have preyed on the Argentinosaurus. It is hard to imagine a Giganotosaurus taking down a 50-tonne Argentinosaurus. Though there is no conclusive proof, a hint of a predator–prey relationship was provided by the discovery of the bones of the Argentinosaurus in the proximity of those of Giganotosaurus.

253 Did you know that the Carcharodontosaurus could have swallowed a human being in one bite? This creature's head was as long as an average human being (about five feet long). The creature was about 44 feet in total length and around 7.5 tonnes in weight. It was thus one of the longest and heaviest known carnivorous dinosaurs.

SAURISCHIAN (LIZARD-HIPPED) DINOSAURS

254 Carcharodontosaurus means 'shark-toothed lizard' or 'jagged-toothed lizard'. It was named after the rough similarity once observed between its teeth and those of the Carcharodon, the great white shark. It had massive jaws equipped with teeth up to 0.2 metres long, which would have slashed through the flesh with ease.

255 The Monolophosaurus had a thick and knobby head crest. This was hollow and may have acted as a means for the dinosaur to produce loud noises, possibly to attract a mate or to warn off a rival. It had a particularly slender lower jaw, but enormous nostrils. It lived in the woodlands of China, in the mid Jurassic period.

256 Due to its stiff tail, the Monolophosaurus is categorised as a Tetanuran Theropod. Its tail was kept straight by a series of tendons and carried off the ground, as is seen in the case of most well-known Theropods, such as the Allosaurus and Tyrannosaurus. While some palaeontologists think that the Monolophosaurus could have been a primitive Tetanuran, others speculate that it belongs to the Neo-Tetanura group.

THEROPODA

257 Sinraptor means 'Chinese thief'. Scientists have found tooth marks on a Sinraptor's skull that seem to have been made by another Sinraptor, which suggests that these dinosaurs may have engaged in vicious fights. Palaeontologists also believe that the Sinraptor was a close relative of the Allosaurus. The Sinraptor also roamed in the woodlands of China in the late Jurassic era.

258 The Gasosaurus means 'gas lizard'. It was so named because it was discovered when a Chinese gas mining company was using dynamite to clear rocks in 1985. Its skull has never been found, so its proposed shape is based on that of other similar dinosaurs.

259 It is interesting that a news piece became the subject of an internet hoax in the year 2014. This news claimed that a '200 million year old' Gasosaurus egg had hatched due to the carelessness of a museum. It further said that the egg was carelessly stored next to the boiler of the museum, due to which somehow the egg managed to incubate and hatch. However, soon people realized that it was not true.

SAURISCHIAN (LIZARD-HIPPED) DINOSAURS

260 Scientists believe that although the Eoraptor had five fingers on each hand, two of those were probably useless. The Eoraptor only had claws on the three longer fingers of its hands. The other two fingers were shorter, stubby and clawless, but probably helped in searching through vegetation for prey.

261 The Eoraptor had an unusual neck — it had a shorter neck than the later carnivorous dinosaurs. Even so, its neck was flexible enough for snatching prey from the ground. It had the blade-like teeth of a carnivore, suitable for slicing through flesh. It mainly hunted small animals but may have taken on bigger prey by tearing out lumps of flesh and waiting for the victim to weaken.

262 Coelophysis is considered to be one of the earliest Theropods. It was small and nimble and resembled a long-legged bird. It was also a bird-like carnivore that darted after prey in the riverside forests of the Triassic period, snapping up prey such as small lizards. It was built for speed, with lightweight, hollow bones and a slender frame.

THEROPODA

263 Did you know that the Coelophysis had a long, flexible neck that formed an S-shape when relaxed, like the neck of a heron? By straightening its neck quickly, it could dart after fast-moving prey on the ground. Its tail was stiff and long and acted like a rudder, helping it balance when running after prey or fleeing from bigger carnivores.

264 Scientists believe that tiny bones found in the stomach of a fossilised Coelophysis were of a baby Coelophysis. They feel this is evidence of cannibalism (the practice of eating members of one's own species). However, some experts counter that the bones were those of some other reptiles that the Coelophysis might have hunted and eaten.

265 Many palaeontologists believe that either the male Coelophysis were bigger than females, or it could be vice-versa. Based on the study of many Coelophysis specimens, palaeontologists established the existence of two basic body plans among these dinosaurs: robust (that is, not so small and slender) and gracile (that is, small and slender).

SAURISCHIAN (LIZARD-HIPPED) DINOSAURS

266

The Coelophysis had unusually large eyes. It is believed that Coelophysis had well-developed eyesight, like many small Theropod dinosaurs of the Mesozoic era. The well-developed eyesight may even be a hint that this dinosaur hunted at night and that it had a comparatively bigger brain, as bigger eyes usually mean a correspondingly bigger brain.

267

The Dubreuillosaurus had an unusually long and shallow skull which was three times longer than it was deep. The skull did not have any distinct crests or horns (like those seen on other dinosaur skulls), but since the only known specimen is of a young Dubreuillosaurus, it can be assumed that these structures might have developed in adults.

268

The Dubreuillosaurus was named in 2002 and was originally thought to be a new species of Poekilopleuron, a large Allosaurus-like Theropod. Later on, a study of its hollow skull showed that the Dubreuillosaurus was more closely related to the Megalosaurids. Like its relatives, it probably had short powerful arms with three-fingered hands, heavily muscled legs and a stiff tail that it held out for balance.

THEROPODA

269 **Spinosaurids were huge, sail-backed dinosaurs that lived in swamps and estuaries.** With their crocodile-like snouts and powerful, clawed hands, they were ideally built for catching the biggest fish of the time. They were also skilled at hunting on land. They had stiff tails that they held out for balance.

270 **Scientists believe that the sail of the Spinosaurus might have had various uses.** Some think it was for display or that it acted as a radiator, helping the Spinosaurus keep cool in the hot climate. Others think the sail was a hump that stored body fat for energy, as in modern camels.

271 **Scientists believe that the Spinosaurus died out in the late Cretaceous period, around 93 million years ago, when the sea levels on Earth dropped and the swamps that the Spinosaurus lived in dried up.** It is also believed that the nostrils set back from the tip of its snout enabled the Spinosaurus to breathe underwater, while hunting for fish.

SAURISCHIAN (LIZARD-HIPPED) DINOSAURS

272 Spinosaurus means 'spine lizard'. This dinosaur got this name because of the enormous sail that ran along its back. This sail was supported by spines made of bones which were as tall as a human. The Spinosaurus was even bigger than the Tyrannosaurus and is one of the largest living land predators of all time.

273 Have you heard of the Irritator dinosaur? Its name came about when clumsy attempts were made to mend the fossil of the dinosaur with plaster. This had irritated the scientists who later tried to undo the damage done to the specimen. It had a short-raised toe at the back of its foot and it also had powerful hind legs. The Irritator used its long teeth to grab and hold on to fish. It may have fed on dead meat, as well as land animals.

274 Baryonyx means 'heavy claw'. The Baryonyx was given this name as a reference to its huge, hook-like thumb claws, which it may have used to spear fish, as grizzly bears do today. You will be amazed to know that remains of partly-digested dinosaurs were found in the Baryonyx's fossilised stomach, indicating that it ate land animals as well as fish.

THEROPODA

275 The Suchomimus had more than a 100 teeth along its jaw that slanted backwards and were pointed like the prongs of a rake. Another set of longer teeth lay clustered at the tip of its snout. It might have used its sharp teeth and snout to catch fish and other slippery prey. Compared to other meat eaters, it had long and powerful arms.

276 Scientists believe that the Allosaurus had deadly teeth. Even though it was a fierce predator, it had a weak jaw that prevented it from crunching bones. It thus depended on its teeth which were like saw blades and could slice through skin and muscle to tear out great ribbons of flesh. Victims that managed to escape after being attacked would probably have bled to death.

277 When young, the Allosaurus was a fast runner and probably actively chased after prey, sprinting on its long and powerful hind limbs. Older ones were heavier and probably relied more on ambushing victims than chasing them down. The long, curved claws on their hands could have been used like meat hooks to capture prey.

SAURISCHIAN (LIZARD-HIPPED) DINOSAURS

278 According to scientists, the Allosaurus had a holey skull: the massive skull had large openings that made it lightweight, yet strong. The bone was also riddled with smaller holes that may have contained air sacs linked to the lungs. It had triangular horns in front of each eye, perhaps for display.

279 The Guanlong was an early Tyrannosauroid. It was much smaller than the later giants and had three fingers on each hand rather than two. It was a close relative of the early feathered dinosaurs and may well have had a coat of fuzzy feathers itself. It had a hollow crest running from the nose to the back of its head.

280 Tyrannosauroids, which means 'tyrant lizards', are among the largest and most terrifying predators of all times. The first Tyrannosauroids were small, possibly feathered dinosaurs; over millions of years they evolved into giants, the largest being the Tyrannosaurus. The giant Tyrannosauroids had immensely powerful jaws lined with bone-crunching fangs, which made them capable of consuming almost any animal they came across.

THEROPODA

281 The jaws of the Albertosaurus were lined with 60 banana-shaped teeth and its head was huge, with triangular horns in front of its eyes. More than 30 specimens of the Albertosaurus have been found, including 22 at a single site that contained a mix of old and young individuals. Some experts think the mass grave is evidence that the Albertosaurus lived and hunted in packs.

282 The Tarbosaurus was typical of the gigantic, late Tyrannosauroids, with a massive skull, powerful jaws and huge, banana-shaped teeth. In contrast, its arms were almost ridiculously tiny and its hands had only two fingers each. It probably crushed its victims in its jaws and then tore off chunks of flesh while holding the carcass down with its feet.

283 The Proceratosaurus is thought to have been a small, early Tyrannosauroid and a close relative of the Guanlong. Its most distinctive feature was a strange crest perched on the tip of its snout. As the top of the skull is missing from the fossils, scientists do not know if the small nose crest was actually part of a much longer crest, like that of a Guanlong.

117

SAURISCHIAN (LIZARD-HIPPED) DINOSAURS

284 You will be amazed to know that Tyrannosaurus had bone-munching teeth. Most of the carnivorous dinosaurs had blade-like teeth with saw tooth edges, but those of the Tyrannosaurus were huge pointed spikes that could pierce the skin, muscles and bones of its prey. Its huge jaws and teeth were specially adapted to eating bones.

285 The Tyrannosaurus had tiny arms and odd hands with just two-clawed fingers each. The arms could not reach the mouths or even each other, but they were very strong. Perhaps the Tyrannosaurus dug its claws into victims while holding them in its mouth to stop them from struggling free.

286 Have you seen the movie *Jurassic Park*? If so, did you know that the lead role in the movie was played by a Tyrannosaurus? The movie *Jurassic Park* confirmed the status of Tyrannosaurus as the most fearsome and famous dinosaur of all. Though not the largest carnivore ever to walk on land, it was the biggest of its time and the strength of its bite was greater than that of any other land animal.

THEROPODA

287 **Can you imagine a dinosaur the size of a chicken?** As hard as it may be to believe, some members of the Compsognathus family were no bigger than chickens. The Compsognathus were nimble little predators that hunted small animals. They were related to the ancestors of birds and probably had simple, fuzzy feathers to keep their small bodies warm.

288 **The long tail of the Compsognathus comprised more than half of its total body length and was used for balance, helping it make sharp turns as it dashed about.** Scientists think soft feathers covered most of its body, especially its back. It is believed that this creature lived in the areas of modern-day Germany and France, in the late Jurassic era, around 150 million years ago.

289 **The Compsognathus had hollow bones that kept its body as light as that of a bird.** Running swiftly on the tips of its toes, this lightweight predator could outpace fast-moving preys, such as lizards, before pouncing upon its victim. It had large eyes, clawed hands and sharp, curved teeth, like those of typical carnivorous dinosaurs, despite its small size.

SAURISCHIAN (LIZARD-HIPPED) DINOSAURS

290 Ornithomimids were also known as 'ostrich dinosaurs'. The members of the Ornithomimidae family were built like ostriches and were just as quick on their feet. They were the fastest dinosaurs of all, capable of reaching speeds of perhaps 80 kilometres per hour (50 miles per hour) when running. They had evolved from flesh eaters, but their bird-like beaks and lack of big teeth suggest a more varied diet.

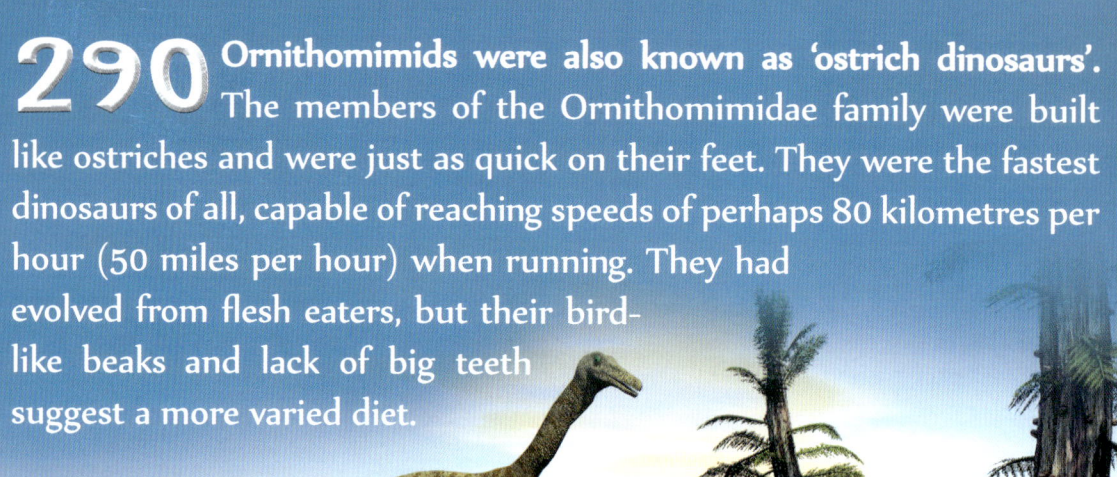

291 It is really interesting to know that the brain of the Gallimimus was about the size of a golf ball (only slightly larger than an ostrich's). The Gallimimus was the largest Ornithomimid, three times as tall as a man and weighing about 450 kilograms. It was the fastest sprinter among dinosaurs and could have outrun a racehorse.

292 The Gallimimus had wide eye sockets with eyes facing sideways. One can say it had bird vision. This helped it spot enemies in almost any direction. It had a supporting ring of small bony plates inside each eyeball. An amazing fact is that modern birds still have this feature.

THEROPODA

293 For many years, scientists mistakenly thought the fossil of the Struthiomimus to be that of the Ornithomimus, as both these species were very similar. The only difference was that the Struthiomimus had longer arms with stronger fingers. At the ends of its fingers were long, straight claws; but it probably could not use them to grasp prey, like the Ornithomimus could.

294 The Ornithomimus had the typical short body and long back legs of an Ornithomimid dinosaur. A fast runner, it could make sudden turns, even while sprinting, by swinging its tail from side to side. For its size and time, it had a fairly large brain but was far less intelligent than an ostrich.

295 The Oviraptorosaurs are a family of odd-looking feathered dinosaurs with parrot-like beaks. Although they evolved from flesh-eating dinosaurs, they are likely to have been either omnivores or plant eaters. They had few or no teeth, short snouts and often a decorative crest on the head. It is also believed that they hatched their eggs by brooding, as birds do today.

SAURISCHIAN (LIZARD-HIPPED) DINOSAURS

296 **The Ingenia had stout hands with unusually large thumbs and thumb claws, which may have been defensive weapons.** This was a small, feathered dinosaur, barely as tall as a man. It may have been an omnivore, feeding on a mix of plant and animal food. It was named after the Ingen Khoboor province in Mongolia, where it was first found.

297 **The Caudipteryx dinosaur was just about the size of a turkey and was covered in feathers.** It had large plumes on its short, wing-like arms, a large tail fan, and short, downy feathers all over. The feathers were probably used to keep it warm and to attract mates rather than to fly.

298 **On the basis of their study, scientists believe that the Therizinosaurs were the most bizarre-looking dinosaurs ever.** They were tall, with small heads, stumpy feet and pot-bellies. While their bones show that they were relatives of predatory dinosaurs, their teeth and digestive system seem to have been meant to eat plants instead of meat.

THEROPODA

299 An interesting fact about the Dromaeosaurus is that its long arms folded up like wings, and its body was fully feathered. These creatures are sometimes called 'raptors'— a word that means 'thief' or 'grabber'. They were small but ferocious hunters with blade-like teeth and vicious, hooked claws on their hands and feet.

300 You may be amazed to know that one fossilised claw of the Utahraptor measures about 0.24 metres (24 centimetres) in length. The Utahraptor was the largest Dromaesaur and reached about half a tonne in weight, making it heavier than a grizzly bear. It had a large, hooked claw on its second toe that it might have used to slash a victim.

301 The Bambiraptor had a very large brain compared to its body size, implying that it was a quick-witted animal. Bambiraptor was bird-like and probably feathered, with long hind limbs that suggest that it was a fast runner. It probably hunted small mammals and reptiles, snatching them in its clawed hands.

SAURISCHIAN (LIZARD-HIPPED) DINOSAURS

302 Did you know, the Troodon had binocular vision? The Troodon's eyes, unlike those of other dinosaurs, faced forward rather than sideways, just like human beings. This enabled the Troodon to judge the distance to its prey before pouncing for the kill.

303 Long, slender legs and an athletic build made the Troodon a fast sprinter, able to outrun small animals, such as lizards and baby dinosaurs. The second toe on each foot had a large, sickle-shaped claw that the Troodon may have used to pin down its prey. Its sharp claw could swivel upwards to stay off the ground while Troodon was running.

304 Troodon eggs were found at Egg Mountain in Montana, USA. Scientists used the tiny bones in a fossil egg to recreate a life-like model of a baby Troodon about to hatch. It appears that both parents sat in egg-filled nests, using their feathered arms to protect the eggs.

THEROPODA

305
Did you know that the Herrerasaurus was one of the earliest dinosaurs? Its name means 'Herrera's lizard', and it was named after the rancher who discovered the first specimen. It was first found in South America. The Herrerasaurus was one among the various kinds of dinosaurs which emerged there roughly 231 million years ago.

306
Categorising the Herrerasaurus was a difficult task for scientists. Scientists spent years trying to classify this odd-looking creature. Some thought it was a Sauropod as it was quite similar to the gigantic, long-necked herbivores. Some others thought it could not even be considered a proper dinosaur but rather as a predecessor to dinosaurs. Finally, it was categorised as a basal Theropod.

307
The Herrerasaurus remains have helped scientists to explain the evolution of modern bird wings. The wrist and lower arm of the Herrerasaurus look fairly unusual for a reptile, yet they do crudely resemble those of 21st century avians. Like a modern pigeon, the forelimbs of the Herrerasaurus utilised a similar range of motion and may have even been decorated with lengthy feathers.

SAURISCHIAN (LIZARD-HIPPED) DINOSAURS

308 The Cryolophosaurus is also known as the 'Elvisaurus'. The reason for its strange name was the head crests that ran parallel to the sides of its skull, a common feature in Theropod dinosaurs. Like a peacock's tail, the crest seems to have been curved, a reminder of the iconic hairstyle of the famous singer, Elvis Presley.

309 Do you know which dinosaur was the first to be officially named? It was the Megalosaurus. Interestingly, both the species of Megalosaurus—M. lydekkeri and M. woodwardi—are considered to be dubious species of the Magnosaurus, due to the limited fossils and lack of identifiable characteristics.

310 It is really interesting to learn that one of the first dinosaurs to be studied and described was the Streptospondylus, though it was not the first to be named. In the year 1808, Cuvier described the Theropod vertebrae of Streptospondylus as the first dinosaur ever. However, at the time, he considered them to be crocodilian in nature.

THEROPODA

311 **The Torvosaurus had an elongated, narrow snout, with a kink in its profile, above its large nostrils.** This kink is really its most distinguishable feature, as generally this area is straight among Theropods. Despite limited fossil remains, the Torvosaurus is believed to have been one of the largest known Theropod dinosaur of the Jurassic era.

312 **The Haplocherius dinosaur belonged to the Alvarezsauroid family.** Unlike others of this family, though, it had three-fingered hands, of which one was an enlarged thumb claw. It is believed that the other two fingers might have been vestigial appendages. It had long legs, so it was probably a fast runner.

313 **Can you believe that there existed dinosaurs that weighed a few grams only?** The weight of the Parvicursor dinosaurs was around 162 grams (0.162 kilograms) and they were only about 0.30 metres (39 centimetres) in length—from the snout to the end of their tail. 'Parvicursor' means 'small runner', and is an apt name as they could run fast due to their long, slender legs. This dinosaur belonged to the Maniraptora family.

SAURISCHIAN (LIZARD-HIPPED) DINOSAURS

314 You will be amazed to know that the Shuvuuia had tiny and rice-shaped teeth. It had a few dozen teeth inside its narrow mouth; but as they were not serrated, it could not eat meat. It was characterised by short but powerful forelimbs specialised for digging. It was a member of the Alvarezsauridae family.

315 One unique trait of Shuvuuia, which is not found in any other non-bird dinosaur, is that it had a hinged upper jaw. In an interesting adaptation, the Shuvuuia could bend its snout upward independently of its skull. This was made possible by special hinges near its eye sockets.

316 Some scientists believe that the Albertonykus might have fed on wood-nesting termites, as the forelimbs of this dinosaur appear to have been specialised for digging, but were too short for burrowing. The fact that dinosaurs like the Alvertonykus existed was unknown until the 1990s. It is the earliest known North American Alvarezsaurid dinosaur.

THEROPODA

317 Generally, in the case of most Theropod dinosaurs, the second finger on each hand is the longest. In the case of the Scansoriopterygid, however, it had an extremely long third finger, which was longer than the first and second fingers. Scansoriopterygidae, which means 'climbing wings', is part of the climbing and gliding Maniraptoran dinosaurs.

318 The Omnivoropterygidae is a family of dinosaurs that had a unique distinguishable feature: these dinosaurs had teeth in the upper jaw but not in the lower jaw. Omnivoropterygidae means 'omnivorous wings'. It was a family of primitive avialans known to be exclusively from the Jiufotang Formation of China. They had short, skeletal tails and unusual skulls.

319 The Tawa was a Theropod dinosaur that was most likely to have eaten meat, whose braincase and neck were surrounded by airsacs, just like in birds found today. It is known to have had multiple specimens, ranging from small juveniles to sub-adults. The name Tawa is derived from the Hopi term for the Puebloan sun god (Puebloans are a sect of the Native American people).

320 The Daemonosaurus Chauliodus is a dinosaur whose name means 'the evil spirit reptile with outstanding teeth'. It dates back to the end of the Triassic period, approximately 205 million years ago. Its huge front teeth would have been useful for seizing and killing prey, and its short and deep snout suggests powerful biting ability.

SAURISCHIAN (LIZARD-HIPPED) DINOSAURS

321 **The transition from five fingers to three can be seen in the hands of the Eodromaeus: its fourth and fifth fingers were much smaller than the first three.** It was a bipedal Theropod with smaller forelimbs, ending in hands. When its remains were first found, scientists had confused it with the Eoraptor, but later, when more fossils were uncovered, it was recognised as being different.

322 **Did you know that the Limusaurus or 'mud lizard' transformed as it aged?** While juvenile Limusaurus had teeth, as they aged these teeth were completely lost and replaced by a beak. Due to this transformation, there probably occurred a shift in their diet with age: from omnivorous to herbivorous.

323 **Scientists believe that the arms and hands of the Limusaurus were considerably reduced, and indicate the trend of moving from five fingered to three fingered Theropods.** The first finger was smaller than the other fingers and lacked digits or sections entirely, while the second had three digits or bone sections. It also had three digits in its third finger as opposed to four, as with other early Theropods.

THEROPODA

324 **The Elaphrosaurus is significant in two ways.** First, for a Theropod of its size, the Elaphrosaurus was very shallow-chested and had a relatively long trunk. Second in comparison to its long trunk, this dinosaur had very short hind limbs. Though it was a Theropod, it had a long neck and was long and slender in shape.

325 **Did you know that the dinosaur known as the Ceratosaurus has been a movie star for over a hundred years?** In the year 1914, audiences watched a reproduction of this species stalk cavemen in *Brute Force*, challenge a Triceratops in *One Million Years B.C.* (1966), and gag at the sight of Spinosaurus faeces in *Jurassic Park III* (2001).

326 **Though a lot can be learnt from fossils, the functions of some of the body structures have been debated at length.** For instance, scientists are not completely sure about the use of the nasal horn of the Ceratosaurus. It is suggested that it could have been used as a powerful weapon for both offensive and defensive purposes. On the other hand, it has also been suggested that it might have just been used for display than for actual defence.

SAURISCHIAN (LIZARD-HIPPED) DINOSAURS

327 One of the most scary features of the Ceratosaurus was that it had unusually long teeth. The upper teeth of the Ceratosaurus were so long that when its maw assumed a closed position, they extended below the lower jaw. Even as a fossil, this is a very impressive feature.

328 A very unusual and striking feature of the Masiakasaurus is the way the front teeth pointed forward and out of the mouth. This created a hooking action as its front teeth curved upwards at the end. This dinosaur had a great ability to catch small, fast moving prey due to this feature.

329 Generally, dinosaurs were named after the palaeontologists who discovered them or the regions they were discovered in. But the Masiakasaurus knopfleri was named after the musician Mark Knopfler, because his music inspired the expedition crew during their explorations. The term Masiaka means 'vicious' in Malagsy; thus, the name of the genus means 'vicious lizard'.

330 It is a really interesting fact that even though the Rajasaurus was a Theropod, it had head ornamentation. Scientists say that even as the dinosaurs of North America lost their head crests in the process of evolution, this feature of head crests began to be seen in the dinosaurs of India.

AVIAN DINOSAURS

Primitive Feather Dinosaur

331 Richard Owen was a palaeontologist who coined the word 'dinosaur' in 1842. The word came from the Greek term meaning 'formidable lizard'. True scientific researches on dinosaurs began in the early 1800s. At that point, these creatures were believed to be related to the reptile family. By the mid-1990s, newer fossils made some scientists consider linkages between dinosaurs and birds.

332 Birds are believed to have evolved from the Theropod group of dinosaurs. Hence, it is sometimes said that all present day birds are feathered dinosaurs. Among the extinct dinosaurs, several of the fossilised remains have been found to have had feathers or feather-like integuments.

AVIAN DINOSAURS

333 **The Archaeopteryx is said to be a close ancestor of the present-day birds.** As a species it is considered to lie between the dinosaurs and the modern birds. Most of the fossils of this huge bird were found with traces of feathers, but we do not know whether it flapped its wings for flying or glided.

334 **Many dinosaurs were found to have feathers on their bodies including the Velociraptor.** However, it has not been possible to determine if the feathers were ever used for true flight. Many scientists believe that the feathers may have been on their bodies to keep them warm. Some also believe that they might have had bright-coloured feathers that were used for mating displays by the males.

335 **In 1995, a scientist named Hou and his colleagues reported findings of a pigeon-sized dinosaur specimen in north-eastern China.** They suggested that the species may have lived before the Archaeopteryx but had similar hind limbs. The skeleton also showed long fingers with long and curved claws and avian-like contour feathers.

Non-Avian Dinosaur with Feathers

336 The presence of feathers has always been used as a defining feature of birds. But there have been discoveries of several non-avian dinosaurs in China where traces of feathers have been found, proving that feathers were not restricted to birds, at least among the dinosaurs.

337 Several non-avian Coelurosaurian Theropods used to have feathers. Coelurosaurs were carnivorous dinosaurs that were only two to three metres long and relatively smaller than other carnivorous dinosaurs. They existed during the mid Triassic time, nearly 230–200 million years ago.

AVIAN DINOSAURS

338 **The Sinosauropteryx is distantly related to birds.** Fossilised remains have given evidence of traces of feathers on the body. Researchers found these feathers to be about 20 millimetres long. They suggested that these were down feathers and were probably used for insulation rather than for flight.

339 Another fossil was discovered in 2009 of a feathered dinosaur. The Beipiaosaurus was reportedly found covered in simpler feathers that would have been 10–15 centimetres long. Interestingly, the feathers on this dinosaur were only present on the head, neck, and tail.

340 **The fossils of the Oviraptorid Caudipteryx and Dromaeosaurid Sinornithosaurus seem to have been more closely related to birds.** They had elongated wings and tail feathers that were structurally identical to the feathers of the birds we find in present times.

NON-AVIAN DINOSAUR WITH FEATHERS

341 One of the families of feathered Theropod dinosaurs was the Dromaeosauridae. This family consisted of small and medium-sized feathered carnivores. They were present in the Cretaceous Period. Researches have shown that at least five Dromaeosaurid species were able to fly or glide.

342 Fossils related to the Dromaeosaurids suggest that they used to hunt in coordinated packs like many of the present day mammals. Some of the researches also revealed that the species may have cooperated and collaborated while hunting. Scientists have also cited other supporting evidences to prove that Dromaeosaurids used to live in groups.

343 Rahonavis ostromi was a non-avian bird from the family of Dromaeosaurids and was believed to have the ability of a powered flight. Its long forelimbs show evidence of quill knob attachments. This is a marker that suggests the presence of sturdy flight feathers. Their forelimbs were also more powerfully built than the Archaeopteryx.

AVIAN DINOSAURS

344 Luis Chiappe studied the flight possibilities of Rahonavis ostromi. Many studies were conducted on this non-avian creature. Chiappe explained that Rahonavis ostromi could possibly fly but unlike the present day birds, it would have been much clumsier in the air.

345 The Microraptor gui is another species of Dromaeosaurid. Studies show that it may have used its well-developed wings for gliding. It had wings on both the fore and hind limbs. Sankar Chatterjee conducted a study in 2005 and said that the tail and hind wings of the Microraptor helped it to control its position and speed while gliding.

346 Another close relative of the Microraptor gui is the Changyuraptor yangi. It was a larger creature as compared to the size of the Microraptor gui. Estimated to be the size of a wild turkey, it is likely to have been one of the largest known flying animals during the Mesozoic era.

NON-AVIAN DINOSAUR WITH FEATHERS

347 Although the Changyuraptor yangi was a large animal, scientists have found indications that it was a glider or a flyer. This is based on their finding four wings and similar limb proportions that are required for gliding in animals like the Microraptor gui.

348 Deinonychus antirrhopus also belongs to the species of Dromaeosaurids and it is also believed to have had partial flight capacities. The young ones in this species had longer arms and strong pectoral girdles, which were absent in the adults. Studies argue that the young ones might have been capable of some kind of flight, but then would have lost their ability once they grew up.

349 The wing feathers of the Zhenyuanlong were aerodynamically shaped and unlike the Archaeopteryx, it did not have long and wide-spanning coverts. Its short arms and size suggested that it was incapable of powered flight, but because of its close relation to the flying ancestors it may have had a capacity for gliding.

AVIAN DINOSAURS

350 Some of the Dromaeosaurids are believed to have been nocturnal predators including the Microraptor and Velociraptor. However, after the discovery of iridescent feathers in the Microraptor fossils, scientists have grown increasingly sceptical about the theories related to its nocturnal behaviour. It is widely argued that iridescent plumage is unlikely to be associated with nocturnal creatures. This theory is based on the characteristics of modern birds.

351 Many of the Dromaesosaurids have been noticed to be diurnal or nocturnal predators but there is also a species of Dromaesosaurid that is inferred to be cathemeral, or active at irregular times during the day and night. For instance, the Sinornithosaurus is said to have been active throughout the day at short intervals, and thus cannot be called a diurnal or a nocturnal creature.

352 Two species of Dromaesosaurids are the Buitreraptor and Unenlagia. The former was active during the Cretaceous period, while the latter flourished during the late Cretaceous period. Both of them were large, ground-dwelling creatures, but their fossils show strong flight adaptations. However, scientists believe that they both may have been too large to actually take off from the ground.

NON-AVIAN DINOSAUR WITH FEATHERS

353 The Pyroraptor lived in the late Cretaceous period. Its fossils were found in 1992 in France. It was a small, bird-like predator that had large curved claws on the second toe of each foot. The claws were 2.5 inches long and could have been used as weapons or climbing aids. The fossils show proof that this creature was covered with feathers and had a long thin tail.

354 Shanag was another creature that lived in the early Cretaceous period. It was a small predatory animal and had the characteristics of both Dromaeosaurids and birds. Gregory S. Paul studied its remains in 2010 and estimated its length to have been 1.5 metres, and weight around five kilograms.

355 The Microraptoria appeared to have flourished around 125 million years ago in China. They had long feathers on their legs and were gliders. The adult specimens of the Microraptoria were less than three feet long and weighed up to one kilogram, making them one of the smallest known dinosaurs.

AVIAN DINOSAURS

356 The Anchiornis huxleyi was the small, feathered dinosaur, and is considered one of the first close relatives between birds and dinosaurs. It was one of the smallest non-avian dinosaurs. The Anchiornis had long wing feathers near the wrist, which made the wing broad in the middle. This meant it was not very well-adapted to flight.

357 The Anchiornis had proportionally long forelimbs, similar to the early avians like the Archaeopteryx. These long forelimbs are known to be helpful for flight. However, the Anchiornis also had long flight feathers on its legs, which might have slowed down its running speed. Like modern birds, the Anchiornis had a complex pattern of colouration across its body and wings.

358 The Troodontidae was a family of bird-like dinosaurs. They became important in the study of the origin of birds because they have similar characteristics as early birds. Some fossils from this family were identified as contemporary to the Archaeopteryx.

NON-AVIAN DINOSAUR WITH FEATHERS

359 **The Jinfengopteryx was a species of the Troodontidae, and its fossils were found in China.** These remains show impressions of feathers, but their hind legs lacked traces of flight feathers. Based on their skull remains, it is believed that they may have been herbivores.

360 **The Jinfengopteryx is considered to be the first Troodontid to preserve evidence of feathers.** However, there is some confusion about whether or not they actually belonged to the family of Troodontidae. As a result, in 2012, scientists suggested it should be called a new subfamily, the Jinfengopteryginae.

361 **Mei was a Troodontid dinosaur that lived during the early Cretaceous period.** It was unearthed in China in 2004. It was a duck-sized dinosaur and its skull had many unique features, including closely spaced teeth in its lower jaw.

362 **The specimen of Mei was well preserved with its snout nestled beneath one of its forelimbs and its legs folded neatly beneath the body.** The posture was similar to the roosting position of modern birds. Therefore, it showed another behavioural similarity between birds and dinosaurs.

Present Day Relatives

363 Birds are said to be the only surviving lineage of dinosaurs that are covered in plumage. Since 1996, palaeontologists have identified around 30 families of non-avian dinosaurs with feathers. Their studies infer that feathers originated at the base of this group before being inherited by birds.

364 Feathers are not just present in avian and non-avian bird-like dinosaurs. Rather, it is argued that even the 30-foot Tyrannosaurs might have been covered in feathers! Studies have shown that it is a possibility that all dinosaur lineages had some kind of feathery or downy body covering.

PRESENT DAY RELATIVES

365 The Sinornithosaurus was a feathered dinosaur that lived about 122 million years ago in the early Cretaceous period. The features of its skull and shoulders were similar to that of the Archaeopteryx and other flying dinosaurs. It was one of the smallest Dromaesaurids, and weighed just around three kilograms.

366 The fossils of the Sinornithosaurus show impressions of feathers on its body. These feathers formed wings, but unlike the wing feathers of flying birds, they lacked certain vital features that could help an animal to fly. Hence, scientists suggested that its feathers might have helped it to glide for short distances after leaping from trees or high areas.

367 Empu Gong and his colleagues studied the Sinornithosaurus as the first identified venomous dinosaur. In 2009, Gong and his team noticed fang-like teeth in the fossil's mid-jaw—a feature seen only in venomous animals. The team therefore believed it to be a predator similar to the modern snake, that could stun its prey with its venom.

AVIAN DINOSAURS

368 The Sinornithosaurus was closely related to the Microraptor and hence, there is a possibility that it was also capable of gliding or perhaps even flying. Comparison of the Sinornithosaurus with modern birds and reptiles based on its eye features indicates that it might have been cathemeral, or active both during the night and day.

369 When the first specimen of the Similicaudipteryx was found, there was no trace of feathers in the fossil remains. However, in 2010, two new specimens were found for the same dinosaur which showed evidence of feathers on its hands and tail, while the rest of the body seemed to be covered in short, downy feathers.

370 While studying the specimens of the Similicaudipteryx, Xu and his colleagues described that the feathers of this animal might have changed with age. For instance, its wing feathers were of little use during its young age, especially since the wings only developed fully with maturity.

PRESENT DAY RELATIVES

371 An interesting kind of Troodontid dinosaur was the Xixiasaurus, that lived in the late Cretaceous period. It belonged to a group of small bird-like dinosaurs. It had all the unique skull features of the Troodontids but its teeth were slightly different from the other family members.

372 The Xixiasaurus was around four feet long and had advanced senses like the other non-avian dinosaurs. It had sickle-shaped claws that helped it while hunting. Its lower jaw had a large number of teeth which suggests that it was likely to have been a carnivore.

373 Another Troodontid was the Byronosaurus that was very similar to Xixiasaurus. It was also a small, bird-like dinosaur, with similar tooth structure as the Xixiasaurus. Its teeth were needle-like, and hence were suitable for catching small prey like birds, lizards, and other small mammals.

AVIAN DINOSAURS

374 **The Zanabazar was another Troodontid from the late Cretaceous period.** Based on the fossil remains, scientists found that it had a skull length of 10.7 inches, which makes it the largest known Asian Troodontid. The only Troodontid larger than the Zanabazar was a single specimen from Alaska that is also classified as a Troodontid.

375 **Saurornithoides were another member of the Troodontid family.** Studies show that it had large eye sockets, meaning it probably had good vision both at night and in day light. It had a low head, sharp teeth and relatively large brain when compared to the other members of the Troodontid family.

376 **The Avialae are a group of dinosaurs whose lineage has been traced down to modern day birds.** The Jeholornis belonged to the family of avialans and lived around 120 million years ago, during the early Cretaceous period. The Jeholornis had only a few small teeth, a long tail, and were about the size of a turkey.

PRESENT DAY RELATIVES

377 The adult length of the Jeholornis was 2.6 feet. They had short but high skulls, with lower jaws that were short, stout, and curved downward. Scientists believe that this was an adaptation for eating seeds. Traces of feathers were only present in two specimens, while tail feathers were seen to be short and pointed.

378 The Sapeornis is another avialan that lived during the early Cretaceous period. The length of this animal was about 30–33 centimetres, excluding the tail feathers. The claws of the Sapeornis were more advanced than that of the Archaeopteryx. They had a large wing span, and at the same time, its arms were as long as its legs.

379 The Caudipteryx lived during the early Cretaceous period. It was the size of a peacock, its overall appearance was remarkably bird-like, and it was completely feathered. However, the feathers present were short, indicating that the animal was most likely flightless.

380 The Omnivoropteryx hailed from a family of flying dinosaurs during the early Cretaceous period. It had small legs that were suitable for perching on branches. Its long wings suggested that it did not need running or jumping to take off into the air.

DINOSAUR EXTINCTION

Causes

381 About 250 million years ago the Earth was very different. It was much warmer and the dominating animals were dinosaurs. Fossil records show that they were found in every continent. Contrary to popular imagination, all dinosaurs were not huge. Some were as small as 20 inches! So, what happened to these creatures? Where and how did they disappear?

382 Although it was commonly believed that dinosaurs are an extinct species with no living relatives, later evidence contradict this belief. Fossils suggest that birds might be descendants of flying dinosaurs! There are other living species related to the dinosaurs as well. But the non-avian (or non-flying) dinosaurs disappeared from Earth about 65 million years ago.

CAUSES

383 **Did you know that the extinction of dinosaurs was accompanied by extinction of many other species of amphibians, animals and plants?** More than half the living species on Earth were wiped out! However, other species of mammals, insects and birds survived. This extinction is also known as the Cretaceous–Paleogene (K–Pg) extinction event or the Cretaceous–Tertiary (K–T) extinction.

384 **The truth is that we are not very sure of what caused this mass-scale disappearance of dinosaurs.** This is because there is no recorded evidence or proof of what actually happened. So, scientists use whatever they can find—such as geographical and fossil evidence—to guess at the reasons. Hence, we have a number of theories on what happened to the dinosaurs.

385 **One theory suggests that dinosaurs became simply too big to survive.** Their big bodies needed massive amounts of food and there was just not enough food available. This led to shortage and then to starvation. But this theory does not explain why many of the smaller dinosaurs and other life forms also perished.

DINOSAUR EXTINCTION

386 The big brain theory suggested that their brain was too small for their big bodies and hence, they simply perished. But this does not explain why they flourished for millions of years. It also does not explain why many plant species also died out during the dinosaur extinction period.

387 Another popular theory was that of a sudden epidemic. This theory proposed that a sudden plague hit the dinosaur population, killing off many species. The plague further spread to animals and other species that fed on these diseased dinosaurs. But this theory again does not explain the extinction of plants that should have remained unaffected by dinosaur diseases.

388 The dominant theory for dinosaur disappearance for years was climate change. The climate when dinosaurs roamed the Earth was tropical—warm and humid. But the Earth was slowly cooling down, with ice forming at polar regions, affecting the cold-blooded dinosaurs. However, others have pointed out that other cold-blooded creatures, like crocodiles survived. In addition, scientists have pointed out that this climate change took time, giving the dinosaurs ample time to adapt.

389 **In 1956, a Russian scientist, Joseph Shklovsky, was the first to come up with the meteor theory.** He proposed that a nearby supernova caused a massive radiation shower that completely wiped out the dinosaurs on Earth. The problem with this theory was twofold: first, it did not explain why some species survived, while others did not. Second, no such evidence of meteors were found at the time.

390 **In 1980, physicist Luis Alvarez and his geologist son Walter Alvarez made a startling discovery when conducting research in Italy.** They found a thick layer of iridium-enriched sediment that was dated to the time of dinosaur extinction. On Earth, iridium is a rare metal. But it is far more common in space, suggesting that this deposition was alien in nature! It could only have come on Earth through a falling meteor or comet.

391 **Initially, there were few takers for Alvarez's theory.** Then many more such sites of iridium deposits were found around the Earth. Later excavations and geological study suggests that the site of the actual impact lies in the Chicxulub crater, buried underneath the Yucatán Peninsula in Mexico. Studies show that this crater was indeed formed just around the time of dinosaur extinction.

DINOSAUR EXTINCTION

392 The Chicxulub crater was discovered by geophysicists Antonio Camargo and Glen Penfield, while looking for petroleum drilling sites. This crater is 180 kilometres wide and 20 kilometres in depth. Scientists estimate that it was created by a 10 kilometres wide comet or asteroid traveling at the speed of 30 kilometres persecond!

393 Do you know what made the scientists so sure that the crater was formed by a massive meteor impact? Apart from the iridium deposits they also found melted rock and fractured crystal. The melted rock and the crystal were signs of a massive explosion and the iridium was the clue on what caused the explosion—a meteor or asteroid!

394 Scientists calculate that the impact's effect was massive—two million times that of a nuclear explosion! Such a massive explosion would have turned the Earth's atmosphere into a virtual oven with fires, massive tsunamis and debris clouding the atmosphere. The shock would also have caused volcanoes and earthquake.

CAUSES

395 An asteroid impact would have resulted in the Earth plunging into darkness, bringing down overall temperatures. This would have destroyed plants, killing any surviving herbivores and later, the carnivores. The tsunamis and volcanoes would have added to the damage. The Chicxulub crater and the iridium deposits were the biggest proof of the impact theory.

396 There is another prevalent theory on dinosaur extinction that is also supported by ample evidence—the volcanism theory. Ancient volcanic beds dating back to 70 million years found across the world show that volcanic eruptions were very common at that time. Scientists believe that the effect of the volcanic eruptions could have been just as catastrophic as that of a meteor impact.

397 One of the biggest eruptions occurred in the Deccan Plateau in India. It covered over 200,000 square miles with lava at a depth exceeding 6,500 feet in some places. These eruptions occurred frequently and would have lasted for as long as one to two million years. The volcano theory would have resulted in a more drawn out extinction period.

DINOSAUR EXTINCTION

398 The supporters of the volcanism theory argue that iridium and fractured crystal that is taken as evidence of the meteor theory are also formed as the result of volcanoes. Iridium, though rare on the Earth's surface, is rich in the Earth's core. Hence, the theory that the iridium deposits could have occurred due to an eruption. The crystal or quartz deposits can also be attributed to the same cause.

399 The effect of the volcanic eruptions would have mirrored the meteor impact. Widespread volcanic activity spewed ash, dust and gas in such high amounts that it actually created a debris-filled atmosphere which blocked sunlight and caused global warming. The greenhouse effect and the effect on vegetation would have wiped out the dinosaur population.

400 Fossil records indicate that while some places show a sudden extinction of dinosaurs, others show a more gradual pattern. In the latter case, dinosaurs seem to have died over a period of time. The drawn out extinction is indicative of the volcanic theory. Eventually scientists settled on two theories—an impact by an extraterrestrial object, like a meteor, or the outcome of a massive volcanic eruption.

Early and Late Birds

401 The only dinosaurs that escaped extinction were the ones that could fly and these were the ancestors of the birds we see today. The earliest birds evolved from small two-legged dinosaurs, but they would still have towered over modern birds. In fact, these early birds were very different from the modern birds

402 Palaeontologists believe that birds descended from two-legged dinosaurs called Theropods. But the idea that birds came from dinosaurs is fairly recent and it only became popular after bird-like fossils were discovered in places like China and South America. This discovery also gave us an insight into the fossils found earlier.

403 The first early bird fossil found was the Archaeopteryx, discovered in the 1860s in Germany. The fossil dates back to 150 million years. Their size ranged from that of magpies to ravens. They had reptilian jaws, three-fingered claws, a reptilian spine with a long, bony tail, and feathers. The last feature is the most conclusive evidence which indicates that they could be the ancestors of birds.

DINOSAUR EXTINCTION

404 For a long time, palaeontologists believed that the Archaeopteryx were the first birds. Even the name means 'first bird'. But there were other scientists who doubted whether it could actually fly. New fossils show that the evolution of birds may have begun much before the Archaeopteryx. Fossils of certain dinosaurs predating the Archaeopteryx seem to have a more direct relationship with modern birds.

405 A major discovery in the study of the origin of birds came when a startling number of bird fossils were found in north-east China. Belonging to an even earlier era, these fossils showed feather like features, which scientists called 'protofeathers'. The fossils were fantastically preserved, giving us a clear picture of bird evolution.

406 Fossil records show that birds did not evolve overnight. Rather, their features started appearing one by one, such as two-limbed walk, feathers, wishbone, and so on, till there was a smooth transition to avian dinosaurs. After that there was a burst of bird evolution. In short, bird evolution was slow to take off, but once it did, it fairly exploded!

EARLY AND LATE BIRDS

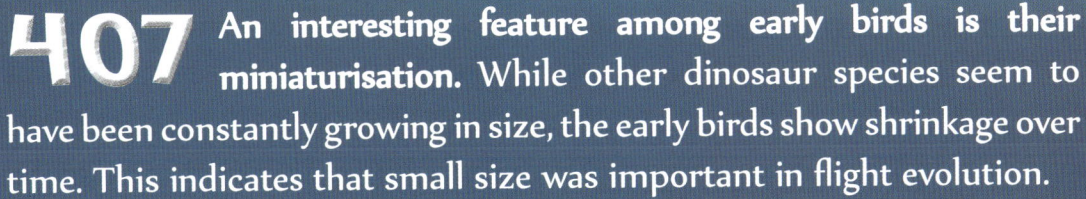

407 An interesting feature among early birds is their miniaturisation. While other dinosaur species seem to have been constantly growing in size, the early birds show shrinkage over time. This indicates that small size was important in flight evolution.

408 Although unable to fly, the Sinosauropteryx is an important fossil in the evolution of birds. It is the first dinosaur fossil that shows evidences of feathers, establishing a link between the dinosaurs and birds. It was small-sized predator that was a very efficient hunter. It also established that even non-avian dinosaurs had feathers.

409 One of the early birds was the Rahonavis. It was a small, approximately 70 centimetres long Theropod. There is a debate over whether it could actually fly or not. The Rahonavis shows both dinosaur and bird-like features. It had long forelimbs, a raised sickle-shaped claw on its second toe, quill knobs and a pelvis that shows adaptation for flight.

DINOSAUR EXTINCTION

410 Paraves includes a wide group in Theropod dinosaurs. Like other Theropods, they walked on their two hind legs. They are divided into two major subgroups: Deinonychosauria, Troodontids and Avialae. They all had winged forelimbs. Some early Paraves had wings on their hind legs as well, earning them the title of 'four-winged dinosaur'.

411 The early Paraves are considered the common ancestor of birds. There are many adaptations that occurred among the different generations of Paravian species. For example, the fingers on the wings fused. The claws disappeared in some later species. The forelimbs grew longer with more feathers, making flight possible. They also shrank in size over generations.

412 One of the most intriguing discoveries of fossils in China was of the Microraptors. These amazingly well-preserved fossils had wings on both forelimb and hind limbs. At just 2.3 kilograms, they were also the world's smallest dinosaurs. They had thick, layered, black feathers that were iridescent. However, some believe that Microraptors were evolutionary dead ends.

EARLY AND LATE BIRDS

413 **Found in Inner Mongolia in 2002, the Scansoriopteryx dates back to 154 million years.** The Scansoriopteryx fossil found was that of a pigeon-sized juvenile. The fossil shows adaptations that include the ability to live on trees. It also had a number of bird-like features, like indications of a membranous wing.

414 **Found in Central Asia, the Longisquama lived about 230 million years ago.** They were quite small, about six inches tall. What makes Longisquama relative to birds is the presence of plumes that jutted out of its vertebrae. Some scientists believe that these were precursors to feathers, while some believe that these appendages were scales.

415 **Found among a nest of eggs, the Oviraptor was first mistakenly called an 'egg thief'.** It was later suggested that it was actually protecting its own egg! It was also once called a bird mimic because this eight feet long dinosaur showed characteristics of a bird. Apart from a feather covered body, it had a sharp toothless beak and possibly a chicken-like wattle!

416 **Dating back to 200 million years ago, the Icarosaurus were found in North America.** These were gliding lizards that could glide over a vast area. They had membranous wings that were stretched over thin bones. These wings were only loosely attached to the animal's body.

DINOSAUR EXTINCTION

417

Pterosaur is a common name for a large class of avian dinosaurs. They showed a wide range in size, from the size of a sparrow to an aeroplane! The Pterosaurs included some of the biggest vertebrates that could fly. Although these flying giants ruled the sky, they are not actually related to the modern bird.

418

The Aerotitans were South American Pterosaurs. These bird-like dinosaurs had long necks with a long cervical vertebra. Some of the Aerotitans were giants with a wingspan of 16.4 feet! Apart from the wings, they also had elongated snouts which gave them a bird-like appearance. However, like the Pterosaur, they had more in common with reptiles than birds.

419

Small and fast, the Velociraptor dates back about 85.8 million years. Despite its feathers and bird-like appearance, the Velociraptor could not actually fly. Palaeontologists see this as proof that some species lost their ability to fly. The Velociraptor could also swivel its wrist and hold its arm against its body like a bird.

420

Named after a flying creature in the movie *Avatar*, the Ikrandraco fossil was found in China. The point of similarity between the fictional creature and the dinosaur is the large keeled crest on its lower jaw. Palaeontologists suggest that it also had a pelican-like pouch on its lower jaw. These flying dinosaurs mainly fed on fish.

Fossil Records

421 We know about dinosaurs through fossil records. But do you know what fossils are? When living things die and decompose, they leave an impression on the rocks or soil. In some cases we have even found intact bodies and plants preserved between layers of soil. The fossils of one era are distinct from fossils above and below. So, we can not only study them, we can also place them in time.

DINOSAUR EXTINCTION

422 We know that dinosaurs had a widespread presence on Earth because we have found their fossils on every continent, including Antarctica. These fossils help us understand the dinosaurs. We use fossilised bones, stomach stones, eggs, soft tissues, internal organs, and even footprints to try and understand their body structure, how they lived, what they ate and what ate them!

423 Interestingly, the idea of dinosaur fossils existed even before they were actually identified and named. There were mentions of dragon bones or giants in legends even before their actual bones were classified. As you know, the term 'dinosauria' came to be used only in 1842, when English palaeontologist Sir Richard Owen used the word to describe his findings.

424 Dinosaurs lived all over the Earth, but still their fossils are not easy to find. Most fossils have been found in the deserts of North America and Argentina. Deserts make an ideal place for fossil preservation because the environment does not allow for other vegetation to cover the samples. The ideal site should also have sedimentary rock layers of the right age.

FOSSIL RECORDS

425 Much of what we know about dinosaurs comes from the Morrison formation, a fertile fossil site in the western US. Stretching from Montana to New Mexico, this rock formation is a rich source of fossils with over 75% of fossils still buried! It gets its name from a place called Morrison in Colorado where the first fossils were discovered.

426 The Morrison formation includes many layers of rock formations, soil and volcanic ash beds. Most of the sediments actually come from rivers, swamps and mudflats. The non-marine dinosaur fossils found here were probably washed up by rivers and deposited on sandbars. This is why most of these were jumbled up and later had to be reconstituted.

427 While the Morrison Formation may have a rich deposit of fossils, the Dinosaur Provincial Park in Alberta, Canada boasts of the largest variety of species found in one site. Dating back 80–70 million years, the site has revealed hundreds of different species. These include Ceratopsians, Parasaurolophus, Euoplocephalus, Troodon, Hadrosaurs, Styracosaurus and Chirostenotes.

DINOSAUR EXTINCTION

428 Situated in Victoria, Australia, right on the ocean-facing cliffs is the Dinosaur Cove. The fossils here date back to 106 million years. At the time of the dinosaurs, this part of Australia was very close to Antarctica. The fossils here provide important clues to the Southern Hemisphere dinosaurs. Among the dinosaurs found here are the 'polar dinosaurs of Australia' that show adaption to polar conditions.

429 Some sites are important because they tell us about the evolution of dinosaurs. The Ghost Ranch in New Mexico is an example of such a place. It is a relatively unchanged flat-lying landscape. Excavations in the 1940s revealed early dinosaurs, including a smaller version of the T-Rex. The fertile site has given us important clues to their evolution.

430 Discovered by accident in 1972, the Dashanpu Formation in south-central China is one of the most important discoveries in dinosaur excavation. The site has revealed more than 8,000 bones, mainly Sauropods. The site is also important for revealing a number of other fossils, including early amphibians, fishes, turtles and crocodiles.

FOSSIL RECORDS

431 For many palaeontologists, the Karoo Basin in South Africa is one of the most important sites for understanding evolutionary history. The fossil sites here give us an invaluable peek into dinosaur life dating back to 200 million years ago. The widespread rock deposits here reveal important evolutionary events, like the origin of many dinosaurs, mammals, tortoises and subsequent extinctions.

432 As we know, a series of stunning discoveries was made in the early 1990s in Liaoning, north-eastern China. These gave us an entirely new perspective on dinosaurs, especially the avian dinosaurs. The site also boasts of rich fossil deposits of other living creatures, such as fish, birds, mammals and amphibians.

433 What makes Liaoning such a special site is the astonishingly well-preserved fossils found here. While most sites produce just a few bones, here palaeontologists found intact skeletons and even soft tissues in some of the fossils! Such a rich fossilisation has enabled palaeontologists to study the interplay of dinosaur communities, their evolution, and even inter-species interactions.

DINOSAUR EXTINCTION

434 Home to the feathered dinosaur Archaeopteryx, the Solnhofen limestone area in Germany offers us one of the richest fossilised ecosystems in the world. Once an archipelago, this area is believed to have been part of a placid lagoon, which formed the perfect site for fossilisation. Although not present in large numbers, the fossils are nevertheless brilliantly preserved.

435 Located in the Gobi Desert in Mongolia, the Flaming Cliffs are one of the world's most inaccessible fossil sites. Discovered by the fossil hunter Roy Chapman Andrews in the 1920s, the site contains fossils that date back to 85 million years ago, including Protoceratops, Velociraptor and Oviraptor. It is most well known for the discovery of dinosaur eggs.

436 The Hell Creek Formation in the western US not only houses important fossil records, it also gives us important clues on dinosaur extinction. The iridium deposits in its layers correspond to the K-T Extinction event that wiped out the dinosaurs. Apart from the late dinosaur species, it is also an important site for fossils of other living beings.

FOSSIL RECORDS

437 Las Hoyas in Spain is known for its well-preserved fossils. Some specimens even contain soft tissues. The beautifully preserved fossils give us important clues about dinosaur characteristics and evolution. Dating back 130 million years, the dinosaurs fossils found here include the Pelecanimimus, Concavenator, Enantiornithines and Ornithomimids. Various arthropods, fish and crocodiles fossils were also found.

438 The almost surreal landscape of the Valle de la Luna in Argentina is the site where some of the oldest dinosaur fossils were found. Dating back to more than 230 million years, the rocks here offer an almost uninterrupted sequence of fossils, giving us important clues on evolution. This was a volcanically active floodplain, rich in vegetation and life forms.

439 The most inaccessible fossil site in the world lies in Antarctica. The presence of these polar fossils show us the wide spread of dinosaurs. The poles were considerably warmer when dinosaurs lived here, but they still underwent months of complete darkness. Interestingly, the dinosaur and marine fossils here show no special adaptations for these conditions.

440 In India, the largest dinosaur fossil site is in Balasinor, Gujarat. Discovered in the 1980s during a geological survey, the site gives us valuable information about the dinosaurs that roamed the subcontinent. Palaeontologists have found at least 13 species of dinosaurs here. Even more remarkable are the number of well-preserved fossilised eggs they found, suggesting a hatchery!

Important Personalities

441 Ever since the first dinosaur bones were discovered, they have roused human curiosity and fascination. But the story of dinosaur study is full of intrigue, wars and adventure. It has scientists, adventurers, painstaking hard work, attention to detail, and even thieves! The best part is that we are still learning about them.

442 The first person to scientifically describe a dinosaur was a minister of the Anglican Church. William Buckland was a geologist and palaeontologist who described the Megalosaurus in an 1824 paper to the Geological Society of London. He described it as a giant reptile. However, he was more of a geologist than a palaeontologist.

IMPORTANT PERSONALITIES

443 Before Georges Cuvier (born in 1769), extinction was considered a mere theory or speculation. But the French naturalist's work established that extinction can in fact happen. Although he did not name dinosaurs, he was among the first to suggest that giant reptiles once lived on earth. It was his work in establishing anatomy and palaeontology that earned him the honour of 'Father of Palaeontology'.

444 Although Charles Darwin was not a palaeontologist, his seminal work on evolution did revolutionise all of life sciences. His work was based on years of painstaking study with samples he had collected from across the world. While some of the early palaeontologists still did not agree with him, his theory of evolution became one of the founding principles in the study of dinosaurs.

445 Born in 1804, Sir Richard Owen was a British comparative anatomist who first came up with the term dinosaur (in Greek 'deinos' means 'terrible' and 'sauros' means 'lizard') in 1842. Although an accomplished man, he is said to have often taken credit for discoveries made by others and got into several altercations and fights with them.

DINOSAUR EXTINCTION

446 Luis Alvarez is credited with one of the most important theories in the history of the Earth—the widespread extinction of life, the K–T event. Interestingly, he was actually an experimental physicist and inventor who won the Nobel Prize for Physics in 1968. He was awarded for his contributions to elementary particle physics.

447 One of the most colourful characters in palaeontology, Roy Chapman Andrews was an American naturalist, explorer and adventurer. He is credited with leading several expeditions to Mongolia and the Gobi Desert in the early 1920s, where he discovered several fossils. His excursions were nothing short of adventures. They still make for a fascinating read.

448 Mary Anning was 12 years old when she found an Ichthyosaur fossil on the English coast in 1811. This was even before dinosaurs were identified. She was not a scientist or trained in any way. Despite this, she found several other fossil bones. She came from a poor family and was forced to sell some of the fossils she collected.

IMPORTANT PERSONALITIES

449 **The Mongolian palaeontologist and geologist Rinchen Barsbold was one of the earliest proponents of the theory that birds evolved from Theropods.** He is acknowledged for his work in the discovery of one of the biggest hauls in dinosaur fossils. He is also credited with highlighting Mongolia in palaeontology and as an authority on Eurasian dinosaurs.

450

The American palaeontologist Robert Bakker has managed to combine science and popular culture. He is the author of *Raptor Red* and *The Dinosaur Heresies*, popular books on dinosaurs and their life. With his work for the movie *Jurassic Park*, Bakker has had a defining influence on popular interest in dinosaurs.

451 **Along with Robert Bakker, Jack Horner is credited with creating popular interest in dinosaurs.** In fact, he was the inspiration behind the character of Dr. Alan Grant in the movie *Jurassic Park*. Apart from other discoveries, he found the nesting grounds of the Hadrosaur, giving us a better understanding of their family life.

DINOSAUR EXTINCTION

452 In true adventure hero style, Roland T. Bird rode on his Harley Davidson motorcycle looking for dinosaur fossils. The American explorer roamed America in his quest and is best known for his discovery of the spectacular Glen Rose Trackway. Set near Paluxy River in Texas, the Trackway is a set of beautifully preserved dinosaur footprints.

453 The son of an Italian sailor, José F. Bonaparte started off collecting fossils with his friends as a child for fun. Despite lack of formal training, Bonaparte grew up to become one of the most prominent South American palaeontologists. He discovered a number of Argentinian fossils. In fact, he is credited with making Argentina one of the most important countries in palaeontology.

454 Such was the flamboyance of the American fossil hunter Barnum Brown that he is known more for his personality than his considerable contributions to fossil discovery in North America! He was part of the expedition that unearthed the first T-Rex fossil. He had an unmatched ability to find and excavate fossils and travelled the world as a fossil hunter.

IMPORTANT PERSONALITIES

455 Born in 1905 in Iowa, USA, Edwin H. Colbert was an eminent palaeontologist and author. He was involved in a number of important fossil discoveries such as excavations in Ghost Ranch, New Mexico. His later discoveries contributed to the theory of continental drift. His book *The Dinosaur Book: The Ruling Reptiles and Their Relatives* made palaeontology much more popular.

456 American palaeontologist Edward Drinker Cope has made several contributions to the field. He published more than 1,400 papers, and discovered and named over 1,000 vertebrate species. An avid fossil hunter, Cope almost lost his entire wealth in the pursuit of science. He also later got involved in a bitter feud with palaeontologist Othniel C. Marsh in what was known as the 'bone wars'.

457 Edward Drinker Cope's rival, Othniel C. Marsh, was an equally eminent palaeontologist, responsible for discovery and description of many of new species. He had also contributed to the development of the theory that birds may have come from dinosaurs. Whereas Edward Cope came from a wealthy family, Marsh's many expeditions were supported by his wealthy uncle, George Peabody.

DINOSAUR EXTINCTION

458 The story of dinosaur fossil hunting is not without its rivalries, but none of these were as enduring or as impactful as the 'bone wars' between palaeontologists Othniel C. Marsh and Edward Drinker Cope. Their rivalry spanned decades—from the 1870s to the 1890s. The two fought bitterly, competing, bribing and even looting as they tried to outdo each other!

459 Born in 1949, Sue Hendrickson became famous for discovering an intact fossil of Tyrannosaurus Rex while on an expedition in South Dakota. The fossil was later named Tyrannosaurus Sue in her honour. Hendrickson was actually a diver and an adventurer. But her discovery of Tyrannosaurus Sue made her an instant celebrity in palaeontology circles.

460 Lawrence M. Lambe was a prominent Canadian palaeontologist and geologist. His work came just after dinosaurs were first described scientifically, triggering off a fossil hunting race. Born in 1863, his work in excavating the fossil beds of Alberta encouraged a lot of interest in the field. So significant are his contributions that the Hadrosaur Lambeosaurus is named after him.

IMPORTANT PERSONALITIES

461 **Born in 1823, Joseph Leidy was a professor of anatomy and natural history.** His interest in palaeontology was only part of his interest in fossil hunting. He discovered and described a number of other living beings as well. In palaeontology, he is known mostly for naming the Hadrosaurus. He was a mentor of E. D. Cope, and as a result, was also involved in the infamous 'bone wars'.

462 **Born in 1937, Dong Zhiming was one of China's leading palaeontologists.** He was involved in a number of Chinese dinosaur excavations, describing many of the country's dinosaurs, such as Sauropods. Among his important expeditions was the Dashanpu Formations where he was later instrumental in building a dinosaur museum.

463 **The British palaeontologist Gideon Mantell was actually an obstetrician by training.** Inspired by Mary Anning's discoveries, he later became passionately interested in geology and palaeontology. He discovered a giant tooth in his home county of Sussex, which he named Iguanodon. He was later involved in discovering a number of other fossils in England as well as writing a book on the geology of Sussex.

DINOSAUR EXTINCTION

464 Among the modern palaeontologists, John H. Ostrom was the first to link dinosaurs with birds (after Othniel C. Marsh proposed the same theory in the 19th century). His theory was prompted by the discovery of a bipedal raptor which displayed some bird-like features. Although accepted widely now, at the time his theory incited a very spirited debate.

465 A disciple of Edward Drinker Cope, Henry Fairfield Osborn was one of America's great palaeontologists. Not only was he part of the American museum and geology establishment, he also led several fossil excavations. He described and named several species. However, his most significant contribution was his work with the American Museum of Natural History where he improved the displays greatly.

466 The British palaeontologist Harry Seeley's most important contribution to palaeontology was his classification of dinosaurs in a paper he published in 1888. Till then palaeontologists were using various means to classify them. Seeley divided them according to pelvic bones and joints into Ornithischians and Saurischians. His classification is used even today.

IMPORTANT PERSONALITIES

467 Born in a German aristocratic family, palaeontologist Ernst Stromer was the first to discover Egyptian dinosaurs. Just before World War-I, he travelled to Egypt where he stumbled upon one of the most amazing discoveries. He found a number of large bones which he later described as Sauropod and Aegyptosaurus, Theropods, Carcharodontosaurus and Spinosaurus. Unfortunately, these fossils were destroyed during World War-II.

468 Born in 1944 in the USA, Patricia Vickers-Rich along with her husband, Tom Rich, is famous for their discovery of dinosaur fossils in Dinosaur Cove, Australia. This was a rich haul of fossils on the southern coast of Australia. Did you know that the palaeontologist couple decided to name the first two dinosaurs they found after their children, and the rest after well-known Australian companies?

DINOSAUR EXTINCTION

469 Although not a palaeontologist by training, Joan Wiffen got the credit for discovering the dinosaurs of New Zealand. She became interested in dinosaurs after a visit to Australia and decided to take up classes on fossils. Wiffen discovered her first dinosaur fossils in 1975 in Northern Hawkes Bay, following it with other fossils later on.

470 In the modern era, the credit for naming the maximum number of dinosaurs goes to the Chinese palaeontologist Xu Xing. He had named 60 species by the time he was 43 years old. He is among the leading palaeontologists of China. His other contributions include his work on avian dinosaurs and studying the evolution of feathers.

Media on Dinosaurs

471 **The human fascination with dinosaurs predates any actual evidence of their existence.** Since the two never co-existed, perhaps this fascination started with the large bones that were periodically found in some places. The legend of dragons and other large reptilian creatures were uncannily like dinosaurs. Folklore creatures, like griffins, some believe, were also references to dinosaurs.

473 **The 19th century was an exciting time in scientific history, with new theories and discoveries telling us about ancient creatures like dinosaurs.** Yet palaeontology and dinosaurs were still largely confined to scientific study. There were hardly any depictions in popular culture. This was despite the infamous 'bone wars' that took place at the time.

472 **Richard Owen created a dinosaur exhibition in the Crystal Palace Park in London.** Unveiled in 1854, the Crystal Palace Dinosaurs exhibited the first sculptures of dinosaurs and other extinct species. Although sometimes inaccurate by our modern understanding, they represented the foremost knowledge of the time.

DINOSAUR EXTINCTION

474 One of the few early mentions of dinosaurs is found in the work of Charles Dickens. The taxidermist Mr Venus in the book, *Our Mutual Friend*, was supposedly based on palaeontologist Richard Owen. In fact, Dickens published Owen's writing in his periodicals *Household Words* and *All the Year Round*. Dinosaurs appear in his novel *Bleak House* where he mentions the Megalosaurus.

475 In the early 1900s, the American artist Charles Robert Knight painted a series of paintings of dinosaurs and other prehistoric animals. His painting *Leaping Laelaps*, painted for the American Museum of Natural History in 1897 is one of the first instances where dinosaurs are shown as active creatures. Amazingly, he was practically blind!

476 Dinosaur fossils were by now catching the public attention. While Knight's paintings were becoming popular in American museums, sculptural displays of dinosaurs also started becoming popular. Fossils and reproductions were made and displayed in museums across the world.

MEDIA ON DINOSAURS

477 Dinosaurs debuted in popular culture as the animated character Gertie. Created by Winsor McCay in 1914, it was not just the first fictional dinosaur on screen, it was also among the first animated characters in history. The 12-minute film showed Gertie as a loveable pet of McCay, quite different from their fearsome reputation today!

478 Gertie, the loveable pet, did not stay as the only dinosaur representative for long. In 1914, D. W. Griffith directed the silent film *Brute Force*. Also known as *The Primitive Man*, the film featured a primitive man, apemen and prehistoric animals, including a Ceratosaurus. It also established the idea of dinosaurs as fearsome, bloodthirsty creatures.

479 After Gertie, comic dinosaurs returned to popular culture in 1988 with the TV show Dino-Riders. Produced as a promotional gimmick for a toy line, it featured fearsome dinosaurs that joined humans and humanoids in a battle in prehistoric Earth. Set in the Marvel universe, it had all the punch and fun of a comic series!

DINOSAUR EXTINCTION

480 Dinosaurs made their presence known as non-cartoon TV figures with the 1974 series *Land of the Lost*. The series traced the adventures of the Marshall family in another universe with a number of characters, including dinosaurs. The series featured the T-Rex among other dinosaur species. The series was rebooted in 1991 and again made into a movie in 2009.

481 The King Kong films were among the first to show a well-crafted action sequence involving dinosaurs. The original 1933 film showed a fierce battle between Kong, a huge ape, and a T-Rex. The 2005 remake showed Kong battling two of them in a thrilling sequence. The film also featured a herd of herbivorous Brontosaurus, giant Sauropods.

482 The animated adventure film *The Land Before Time* brought together big names like Steven Spielberg, Frank Marshall, George Lucas and Kathleen Kennedy. The film, set in the universe of dinosaurs, explored a deeper theme of prejudice. Released worldwide in 1988, it was a huge success, resulting in sequels, TV series, as well as dino toys and games!

MEDIA ON DINOSAURS

483 One of the dinosaurs in popular culture is Reptar, depicting a pop culture figure in the Rugrats universe. It is a green glowing T-Rex, revered by children. As a popular character it also has merchandise and amusement parks. It is a particular favourite of Tommy Pickles and his friends in the series *Rugrats*.

484 The 2000 Disney film, *Dinosaur*, featured an orphaned Iguanodon. The makers claimed that the CGI effects and the real world background in an animated film made it a classic. Indeed, the film featured realistic landscape along with realistically depicted dinosaurs.

DINOSAUR EXTINCTION

485 Perhaps the most impressive movie on dinosaurs was a documentary created by Tim Haines for the BBC. Made in 2013, *Walking with Dinosaurs* was a six-part documentary series. The film used CGI and animation to create a completely realistic prehistoric world. Palaeontologists were consulted throughout to ensure scientific accuracy. The result was a highly acclaimed, award winning series.

486 *Godzilla* first came to our attention as a Japanese film made in 1954. Originally conceived as a sort of 'sea monster' the Godzilla was supposedly a mutated dinosaur. It went on to become an iconic pop culture figure with Hollywood remakes, comic books, computer games, toys and other merchandise. However, no one knows what sort of radioactive dinosaur it is supposed to be!

487 For children, perhaps the most recognisable and adored dinosaur is Rex from the Toy Story franchise. Initially appearing in a small role, Rex plays a much larger role in the rest of the movies in the series. It is a toy plastic dinosaur that is given a fictional name of Partysaurus Rex. Insecure about its lack of ferociousness, Rex is often annoying.

MEDIA ON DINOSAURS

488 Dinosaurs appear in the universe as Dinobots. A kind of autobots, they transform into dinosaurs. They are portrayed as fiercely independent, strong and able to fight in robot mode. In the Transformers universe their creation was inspired by dinosaur bones. The Dinobots are led by Grimlock.

489 Set in the Stone Ages, *The Flintstones* featured a number of dinosaurs, including the pet Dino. First appearing as a TV series, the show has had many spin-offs and movies. Dino was portrayed as a loveable pet, faithful and excitable, it often offered comic relief. The movie featured a number of other 'working' dinosaurs.

DINOSAUR EXTINCTION

490 In 1993 came a movie that would forever change the way dinosaurs were seen. With groundbreaking special effects, *Jurassic Park* grabbed immediate attention. This hugely popular film had many sequels, spin-offs and merchandise. But more important than that was its effect on popular culture. It revived interest in dinosaurs and palaeontology worldwide, like never before.

491 Dinosaurs have been a favourite subject for many books, especially for children. Many imaginative stories, novels, comic books and informative books feature dinosaurs as the main character. The fact that they existed much before human beings did and the mystery surrounding their existence and extinction, has triggered the collective imagination of people world over.

MEDIA ON DINOSAURS

492 Compiled by by Dougual Dixon, *The World Encyclopaedia of Dinosaurs & Prehistoric Creatures,* is considered a groundbreaking book for its careful and detailed records of dinosaurs and other prehistoric creatures. The book compiles data from various discoveries and fossil finds in the last two centuries.

493 Published in 2008, written by Australian palaeontologist John A. Long and illustrated by Peter Schouten, *Feathered Dinosaurs: The Origin of Birds,* is a visual record of dinosaurs' evolution to birds. The book is important for its accurate, detailed and engaging descriptions, coupled with equally accurate and stunning illustrations.

494 Released in 1912, The Lost World is a novel written by Sir Arthur Conan Doyle. The story is set in a fictional island in Venezuela where many prehistoric creatures including dinosaurs still co-exist with humans. This novel is remarkable not just for its story, but for the inspiration it provided for later books and movies.

DINOSAUR EXTINCTION

495 Compiling the writings of some of the world's leading palaeontologists, *The Complete Dinosaur (Life of the Past)*, chronicles our understanding of the dinosaurs—from discoveries, findings and theories. At places, the book presents opposing point of views, letting the reader decide. With its beautiful illustrations, it is considered one of the best informative books on dinosaurs.

496 Bringing together the sci-fi writer's love of dinosaurs, *Dinosaur Tales* by Ray Bradbury is a collection of some of his best stories on these prehistoric creatures. The stories include, *A Sound of Thunder, The Fog Horn, Tyranosaurus Rex* and *What If I Said: The Dinosaur's Not Dead?* The collection carries a foreword by animator Ray Harryhausen.

MEDIA ON DINOSAURS

497 The novel, *End of an Era*, written by Robert J. Sawyer is counted among the best works of fiction in dinosaur literature. Released in 1994, it centres a round a couple of palaeontologists who travel back in time to find out what happened to the dinosaurs. They find that the dinosaurs were under the mind control of Martians!

498 The book that sparked off one of the biggest grossing movies of all time was *Jurassic Park* by Michael Crichton. It is just as enjoyable as the movie. Set in an amusement park on an island with resurrected dinosaurs, the book was also a cautionary tale against genetic engineering. Crichton later released a sequel, *The Lost World*, both of which were adapted for movies.

DINOSAUR EXTINCTION

499 If you were ever curious about the T-Rex, simply grab a copy of *Tyrannosaurus Rex: The Tyrant King* to find an answer to all your questions. With contributions from a number of palaeontologists, it is a definitive guide to the apex predator of its time. From its anatomy to the time it lived in, the book is very detailed.

500 The release of *Footprints of Thunder* in 1995 by James F. David started the *Thunder Series*. In the novel a temporal inconsistency blends the contemporary world with the prehistoric world. Dinosaurs invade human cities and towns and a thrilling sequence of events follows. The book even has a T-Rex living on the moon!